Universal Design for Learning
in the Classroom

WHAT WORKS FOR SPECIAL-NEEDS LEARNERS

Karen R. Harris and Steve Graham,
Editors

Strategy Instruction for Students with Learning Disabilities
Robert Reid and Torri Ortiz Lienemann

Teaching Mathematics to Middle School Students with Learning Difficulties
Marjorie Montague and Asha K. Jitendra, Editors

Teaching Word Recognition:
Effective Strategies for Students with Learning Difficulties
Rollanda E. O'Connor

Teaching Reading Comprehension to Students
with Learning Difficulties
Janette K. Klingner, Sharon Vaughn, and Alison Boardman

Promoting Self-Determination in Students
with Developmental Disabilities
*Michael L. Wehmeyer with Martin Agran, Carolyn Hughes,
James E. Martin, Dennis E. Mithaug, and Susan B. Palmer*

Instructional Practices for Students with Behavioral Disorders:
Strategies for Reading, Writing, and Math
J. Ron Nelson, Gregory J. Benner, and Paul Mooney

Working with Families of Young Children with Special Needs
R. A. McWilliam, Editor

Promoting Executive Function in the Classroom
Lynn Meltzer

Managing Challenging Behaviors in Schools:
Research-Based Strategies That Work
*Kathleen Lynne Lane, Holly Mariah Menzies, Allison L. Bruhn,
and Mary Crnobori*

Explicit Instruction: Effective and Efficient Teaching
Anita L. Archer and Charles A. Hughes

Teacher's Guide to ADHD
Robert Reid and Joseph Johnson

Universal Design for Learning in the Classroom

Practical Applications

Edited by

Tracey E. Hall
Anne Meyer
David H. Rose

THE GUILFORD PRESS
New York   London

© 2012 The Guilford Press
A Division of Guilford Publications, Inc.
72 Spring Street, New York, NY 10012
www.guilford.com

Printed in the United States of America

This book is printed on acid-free paper.

Last digit is print number: 9 8 7 6 5 4

Library of Congress Cataloging-in-Publication Data

Universal design for learning in the classroom : practical applications / edited by Tracey
E. Hall, Anne Meyer, David H. Rose.
    p. cm. — (What works for special-needs learners)
    Includes bibliographical references and index.
    ISBN 978-1-4625-0631-6 (pbk.) — ISBN 978-1-4625-0635-4 (hardcover)
    1. Individualized instruction.   2. Cognitive styles.   3. Children with disabilities—
Education.   I. Hall, Tracey E.   II. Meyer, Anne, Ed. D.   III. Rose, David H.
(David Howard)
    LB1031.U52 2012
    371.39′4—dc23
                                                                2012019460

About the Editors

Tracey E. Hall, PhD, is Senior Research Scientist at CAST, a not-for-profit research and development organization whose mission is to improve education for all learners through innovative uses of multimedia technology and contemporary research in the cognitive neurosciences. At CAST, Dr. Hall specializes in alternative assessment and instructional design grounded in effective teaching practices. These experiences are applied in the development and implementation of Universal Design for Learning (UDL) projects, collaborative partnerships, and professional presentations. Dr. Hall brings to her work at CAST more than two decades of experience in the areas of curriculum-based measurement, teacher professional development, special-needs instruction and curriculum design, progress monitoring, and large-scale assessments. She directs CAST's initiatives to create and evaluate digitally supported environments across content areas. She is also Principal or Co-Principal Investigator on several federal- and foundation-funded grants. From 1999 to 2004, Dr. Hall served as director of curriculum for the National Center on Accessing the General Curriculum. A frequent presenter at national and international education conferences, she has taught courses on special education reading and writing, learning disabilities, and behavior management. She has been a special education teacher, consultant, administrator, and university professor, and has consulted at the national and international levels. Before joining CAST, Dr. Hall was Assistant Professor at The Pennsylvania State University in the Department of Educational and School Psychology and Special Education.

Anne Meyer, EdD, is a licensed clinical psychologist and CAST's Chief of Education Design and Co-Founder. Drawing on her long-term focus on the psychological aspects of learning and learning disabilities, Dr. Meyer plays a leading role in CAST's design of multimedia technology for diverse learners. She has also led efforts to refine and disseminate CAST's ideas about UDL through writing and website development. Dr. Meyer is a coauthor (with David H. Rose) of three books—*A Practical Reader in Universal Design for Learning,* the seminal *Teaching Every Student in the Digital Age: Universal Design for Learning,* and *Learning to Read in the Computer Age*—as well as numerous journal articles. She is also coeditor (with David H. Rose and Chuck Hitchcock) of *The Universally Designed Classroom: Accessible Curriculum and Digital Technologies*. Widely recognized for her contributions in the field of technology as it relates to disabilities, Dr. Meyer has served on the Texas Task Force on Electronic Textbook Accessibility and as a national advisor to President Clinton's Educational Technology Panel. In 1995, Dr. Meyer received a Gold Medal from the National Association of Social Sciences for her work at CAST. With her CAST colleagues, she is also a winner of the Computerworld/Smithsonian Innovation Award for the early literacy software program WiggleWorks.

David H. Rose, EdD, is CAST's Chief Education Officer and Co-Founder. He is a developmental neuropsychologist and educator whose primary focus is on the development of new technologies for learning. In 1984, Dr. Rose co-founded CAST; its work has grown into the field of UDL, which now influences educational policy and practice throughout the United States and beyond. Dr. Rose has also taught for more than 25 years at Harvard's Graduate School of Education. In 2009–2010, he served on the technical working group that wrote the National Education Technology Plan for the U.S. Department of Education. As a researcher, Dr. Rose is the Principal Investigator on a number of U.S. Department of Education and National Science Foundation grants, and is currently the Principal Investigator of two national centers created to develop and implement the National Instructional Materials Accessibility Standard. With the increasing prominence of UDL as a field within education, Dr. Rose has become a frequent keynote speaker at national and international conferences. He is the coauthor or coeditor (with Anne Meyer and Chuck Hitchcock) of the books described above in Dr. Meyer's biography. Dr. Rose also leads or participates in many of CAST's technology and media development projects that have resulted in award-winning classroom products, including WiggleWorks. With his CAST colleagues, he has won numerous awards, including the Computerworld/Smithsonian Award for Innovation in Education and Academia (Laureate, 1993; Finalist, 1999), the Tech Museum of Innovation Award (2002), the LD Access Foundation Innovation Award (1999), and the EdNET HERO Award (2005). In 2004, the George Lucas Educational Foundation's *Edutopia* magazine named him one of education's "Daring Dozen."

Contributors

Emiliano Ayala, PhD, is Associate Professor and Chair of the Department of Educational Leadership and Special Education at Sonoma State University. Dr. Ayala teaches and writes about the impact of cultural diversity in education; collaboration and legal issues in special education; and Universal Design for Learning (UDL) in higher education. In addition to his teaching responsibilities, Dr. Ayala serves as Project Director for EnACT~PTD. This U.S. Department of Education grant is designed to support professional development activities for faculty and administrators at institutions of higher education, with the goal of providing a high-quality postsecondary education for students with disabilities.

Michael Barnett, PhD, is Associate Professor of Science Education and Technology in the Lynch School of Education at Boston College. He has led several projects funded by the National Science Foundation. He is also Principal Investigator on several Hewlett-Packard Foundation Teaching with Technology projects and several Massachusetts Department of Education teacher professional development grants. All of these grants have focused on how to support students and beginning teachers in learning science through the use of innovative technologies such as educational video games, geographic information systems, and LEGO Robotics. Dr. Barnett has also served as an assistant regional editor for the *International Journal of Science Education* and currently serves on the editorial board for the *Journal of Science Education and Technology.*

Kati Blair, EdM, is Education Program Manager at VSA Arts of Massachusetts, where she is responsible for developing and documenting effective teaching artist residencies. These residencies help provide the opportunity for collaboration with classroom teachers to create arts-integrated learning experiences for students of all abilities. She also has developed and conducts professional development opportunities for teaching artists, teachers, parents, and professionals about the role of the arts in education to support inclusive practices. Ms. Blair has also taught visual arts to students (K–12) in public schools, museums, and community centers, and designed and implemented arts and mathematics integrated curricula in public schools in Florida. She is also a visual artist and has exhibited work at the Fuller Craft Museum, the Somerville Museum, and the Edinburgh College of Art, and she served as an evaluation consultant for education programs in Boston for the NPR radio show *From the Top.*

Heather J. Brace, PhD, is Assistant Professor of Special Education in the Department of Education and Child Development at Whittier College. Her research interests include the lived experiences of culturally and linguistically diverse families of children with autism spectrum disorders, and the implications of service accessibility for diverse populations.

Jacob Brookover, EdM, was a software developer for CAST from 2009 to 2011, working to integrate UDL into learning environments. His background in secondary education and technology has led to an interest in the relationship between learning and engagement, with a focus on the engaging features of commercial video games. He has taught mathematics and computer science for the Department of Defense Schools in Japan. He has been a consultant to Harvard's Advanced Leadership Initiative, where he designed a computer game to promote ethics; has worked as a Teaching Fellow at the Harvard Graduate School of Education; and has chaired a high school mathematics department.

Bridget Dalton, EdD, is Assistant Professor of Language, Literacy, and Culture at Vanderbilt University's Peabody College of Education. Her research interests focus on literacy and technology, and on students who struggle to learn in today's schools. Before joining Vanderbilt, she served as Chief Officer of Literacy and Technology for CAST and as Associate Professor at the University of Guam. Dr. Dalton has been a coeditor of the International Reading Association's electronic journal *readingonline.org*, and has numerous publications.

Yvonne Domings, EdM, is an Instructional Designer and Research Associate at CAST, where she participates in the formative development and research of technology-based UDL environments. In addition to this work, she creates and delivers professional development programs to integrate UDL into the classroom. Before joining CAST in 2008, Ms. Domings worked in a Massachusetts school district helping teachers broaden regular education curricula to encompass the academic, social, and behavioral needs of students with autism spectrum disorders.

Patricia Ganley, MEd, manages the National Center on Universal Design for Learning, a CAST program that supports the effective implementation of UDL in policy, research, and practice. Ms. Ganley is also Senior Product Development Manager at CAST, where she supports the school-based implementation of research and development projects, including teacher training, classroom instruction, and data collection in classrooms. In this role, she collaborates with teachers, programmers, researchers, and students to develop technology solutions for these projects, bringing to this work more than two decades of experience in education and psychology.

Don Glass, PhD, was a 2010–2011 UDL Fellow at CAST and Boston College. Before that, he was Director of Outcomes and Evaluation for the VSA program at the John F. Kennedy Center for the Performing Arts in Washington, DC. Dr. Glass comes from a background of arts, education, and evaluation to assist teachers in engaging students in creative, collaborative, and authentic learning experiences. He has taken the lead in conducting evaluation research and inservice professional development to translate UDL into practice with the arts, as a mechanism to provide both low- and high-tech learning opportunities.

David Gordon, MFA, has been CAST's Director of Strategic Communications since 2004. He is the editor or coeditor of four books about education, including *A Nation Reformed?: American Education 20 Years after "A Nation at Risk"* and *The Digital Classroom: How Technology Is Changing the Way We Teach and Learn*. From 1999 to 2004, he edited the award-winning *Harvard Education Letter*, winning a National Press Club Award for distinguished reporting and analysis of the national board certification program for teachers. He has taught writing at Emerson College (1998–1999) and served as a staff researcher, writer, and associate editor at *Newsweek* (1989–1997).

Jenna W. Gravel, EdM, is a doctoral student in the Education Policy, Leadership, and Instructional Practice program at Harvard Graduate School of Education. From 2006 to 2010, she was a Research Associate at CAST, where she played a central role in the development of CAST's UDL Guidelines. She is interested in exploring effective implementation of UDL and the impact of the UDL framework on student learning. She is a coeditor (with David Gordon and Laura Schifter) of *A Policy Reader in Universal Design for Learning*. She has been a middle school inclusion specialist in Malden, Massachusetts, and is certified in PreK–12 special education.

Tracey E. Hall, PhD (*see* "About the Editors").

Mindy Johnson, EdM, is an Instructional Designer and Research Associate at CAST, where she helps develop and research technology-based learning environments based on the UDL principles. Prior to joining CAST, Ms. Johnson was a high school special education teacher in Chapel Hill, North Carolina, providing direct instruction to special-needs students and co-teaching in inclusive classrooms with content-area teachers. As a graduate student, she twice won awards for Distinction in Teaching as head teaching fellow for an undergraduate psychology course at Harvard College. Ms. Johnson also works at the Boston Museum of Science as an instructor and mentor, planning and conducting hands-on science workshops and activities for elementary school-age children.

Scott Lapinski, MEd, is a Research Associate at CAST. He plays a key role at the National UDL Center, where he writes and edits reports, literature reviews, and other website content. He also supports the UDL Guidelines project, collecting and analyzing qualitative and quantitative data on how the Guidelines are used. He helped to prepare Version 2.0 of the Guidelines. Mr. Lapinski also contributes significantly to CAST's publications, and is a contributor to three current book projects as well as scholarly articles. Before joining CAST, he worked as an elementary school teacher in Massachusetts.

Anne Meyer, EdD (*see* "About the Editors").

Elizabeth Murray, ScD, is Senior Research Scientist and Instructional Designer at CAST. In this role, she combines her technology skills, special education experience, math expertise, and clinical specialties in applying UDL to technology-based educational materials and instruction through both research and professional development. She has served as Co-Principal Investigator on several federally funded projects that focus on the application of UDL to math curricula and instruction.

Jeremy Forest Price, PhD, is Postdoctoral Scholar at the Lawrence Hall of Science, University of California, Berkeley. He has been helping to write and research the implementation of an urban ecology curriculum intended for nationwide distribution. Dr. Price previously was a Learning and Media Specialist at CAST, where he participated in the design of digital environments that were built upon the UDL principles.

C. Patrick Proctor, EdD, is Assistant Professor of Bilingualism and Literacy at Boston College's Lynch School of Education. He is a former bilingual classroom teacher, and his work focuses on the literacy development of children from immigrant and bilingual homes. His work ranges from theoretical and cognitive conceptions of bilingual literacy development, to applied intervention work in urban classrooms that targets improving reading comprehension and vocabulary development among culturally and linguistically diverse learners. Dr. Proctor's current work takes a developmental perspective on comprehension and vocabulary knowledge among Spanish–English bilingual and English monolingual learners, with an eye toward those instructional practices that affect learning trajectories from second through fifth grades.

Kristin H. Robinson, MA, MPhil, is an Instructional Designer and Research Associate at CAST, which she joined after graduate work and teaching in American studies. Her interests include technology and comprehension; multimedia inquiry and composition; and the design of supported, scaffolded learning environments.

David H. Rose, EdD (*see* "About the Editors").

Skip Stahl, MS, is Senior Policy Analyst at CAST. He is also Project Director of the federally funded NIMAS Center and Project Director for the Advisory Commission on Accessible Instructional Materials in Postsecondary Education for Students with Disabilities—both national initiatives implementing the transformation of academic textbooks into specialized accessible formats for students with print disabilities. As a nationally recognized expert in accessible digital materials and UDL, he has extensive experience in the development of technical standards related to accessible instructional materials, technical assistance to states, and professional development for educators. In addition to his leadership of the NIMAS Center, Mr. Stahl works with policy advocates for educational and instructional materials to ensure that instructional materials are accessible, appropriate, and readily available to all students. He has consulted with software and curriculum publishers in accessible product design and is a nationally recognized conference presenter.

Ge Vue, EdM, is an Instructional Designer and Research Associate at CAST. He is interested in developing social learning technologies and is instrumental in the development of UDL digital literacy environments to support reading, writing, and assessment. He is also interested in the creative use of emerging technology to create flexible learning environments.

Preface

When we were invited to develop a book for this series, our discussions with the series editors initially centered on technology and special education. We quickly realized (and the editors agreed) that this approach would not be helpful for practitioners, but that a book on Universal Design for Learning (UDL) *would* be helpful to guide educators in using a variety of means and methods to meet the needs of all learners. Technology and the special needs of learners are critical themes in this book, but the larger theme is improving education for all by designing learning environments from the outset that are flexible enough for all. Using technology alone—or narrowly addressing the needs of certain populations of students—cannot accomplish this.

We know that new technologies in general and digital media in particular hold enormous promise for improving educational opportunities for all students, but especially those with special needs. When designed well, digital media can (in contrast to print) be transformed, networked, and customized to meet the needs of individual learners and broaden the instructional palette of classroom practitioners.

Yet, as many skeptics of technology in education point out, the promise and potential of new technologies to transform education have yet to be realized. Why? In part, new technologies are not implemented in a curriculum that is designed to meet the needs of all learners. To be effective, technology-based learning needs to take place within a universally designed curriculum—one whose goals, assessments, methods, and materials support student learning through multiple means of representation, expression/action, and engagement.

The UDL Guidelines referred to throughout this book provide teachers with fresh ideas for how to extend learning opportunities to all students. In addition to providing practical information, this book will help educators understand the field growing up around UDL. States, provinces, and individual school districts across the United States and Canada are turning to UDL as a means of helping educators meet the demand to provide standards-based education to all learners, while recognizing and honoring individual variability and diversity. The U.S. Department of Education, the National Science Foundation, and major foundations and corporations are supporting initiatives to expand our understanding of UDL and its transformative potential. The U.S. Congress, in the Higher Education Opportunity Act (HEOA; Public Law 110-315, August 14, 2008), tied funding for teacher professional development and preservice education to UDL implementation. UDL was defined by the HEOA as

> a scientifically valid framework for guiding educational practice that—(A) provides flexibility in the ways information is presented, in the ways students respond or demonstrate knowledge and skills, and in the ways students are engaged; and
>   (B) reduces barriers in instruction, provides appropriate accommodations, supports, and challenges, and maintains high achievement expectations for all students, including students with disabilities and students who are limited English proficient.

The chapters that follow push beyond the lingo and jargon of research and policy to provide classroom-based suggestions and examples of ways to realize the aspirations of UDL in everyday settings. We asked our authors to identify real-world challenges and barriers to implementation, and to provide suggestions for how to overcome those challenges. We also asked them to provide a mix of insights from both research and practice, in the belief that education researchers and practitioners should be talking to and learning from each other—much as they are now doing in medicine, science, business, and other professions.

OVERVIEW OF THIS VOLUME

In Chapter 1, we three editors of this book (Hall, Meyer, and Rose) offer a brief introduction to UDL in question-and-answer format. This introduction covers some of the most common questions about UDL: How does UDL relate to technology? What is the difference between UDL and universal design (UD) in general? And how does UDL apply to the curriculum? This chapter, along with Chapter 2, provides the background knowledge necessary to understand Chapters 3–8, which focus on applying UDL to specific subject areas.

Chapter 2, by Lapinski, Gravel, and Rose, describes the UDL Guidelines—a set of practical checkpoints that help educators carefully plan and structure curricula (including goals, assessments, methods, and materials). The Guidelines are specific and detailed about ways to ensure that all students have the appropriate challenges and supports they need to become accomplished learners. In addition to serving as planning tools, they can also be used for evaluation and lesson study—means of assessing and discussing practice from a UDL perspective.

Beginning with Chapter 3, the discussion turns to more specific skills, content, and subject matter. In Chapter 3, Gordon, Proctor, and Dalton describe a decade's worth of research in how UDL and reading comprehension strategy instruction can be blended with digital learning environments to improve reading for all learners. These authors describe ways that UDL and digital texts can support all learners, and discuss some free, teacher-ready tools for doing so. Chapter 4 addresses writing instruction through a similar lens. Vue and Hall discuss their experiences in working with classroom teachers to develop online supported writing environments based on UDL principles. This work, spurred by the teachers themselves, scaffolds the process approach to writing ("clarify, precompose, compose, publish") in a digital environment. The authors also discuss using the UDL Guidelines to make writing instruction more effective for writers at all skill levels and to make the process more engaging.

Chapters 5–8 describe ways to apply the three UDL principles and the UDL Guidelines to teaching and learning in science, math, history, and the arts, respectively. In Chapter 5, Price, Johnson, and Barnett look at how UDL supports learners in thinking about, talking about, and doing science. In Chapter 6, Murray and Brookover discuss how UDL supports better mathematics instruction in the areas of conceptual understanding, procedural fluency, strategic competence, and adaptive reasoning. In Chapter 7, Robinson and Meyer examine efforts to design a problem-based, inquiry-centered approach to history learning, using the UDL principles. And in Chapter 8, Glass, Blair, and Ganley examine how the arts, including painting and dance, can support UDL implementation. In addition to discussing specific projects and classroom interventions that the authors have worked on, these chapters also point educators to a number of helpful resources (mostly available online for free) to jump-start the process of implementing UDL.

In Chapter 9, Rose, Gravel, and Domings discuss UDL "unplugged"—the application of these principles in low- or no-tech settings. Over the years, many teachers have asked whether they can "do" UDL if they don't have access to state-of-the-art technology. The authors acknowledge the desirability of leading-edge technology, since it is more flexible than older technologies such as pen, paper, and printed text. And this flexibility makes it easier and more cost-effective to include more learners in the educational process. Still, they note: "UDL sets out principles that are focused on teaching and learning, not on the technologies—either ancient or modern—with which those principles are realized" (p. 120).

In Chapter 10, Ayala, Brace, and Stahl consider what the new national emphasis on UDL means for teaching preparation and professional development. They explore the ways in which one California state university is incorporating UDL into its teacher prep program, with an eye toward preparing the next generation of teachers to plan from the outset to meet the needs of all learners.

This book offers invaluable insights from research and practice on how to improve learning for all students through UDL. But of course the educators who read this book will discover their own insights and best practices as they apply the UDL Guidelines to their own classrooms. A central theme of this work is that human variability and diversity are endless, and so our approaches to education must be flexible enough to give everyone optimal opportunities to learn. In short, the great differences among learners and teachers alike are not barriers to be overcome but wonderful strengths to be celebrated and built upon in making education more effective for all.

ACKNOWLEDGMENTS

We are so grateful to Karen R. Harris and Steve Graham for inviting us to develop this book and join the very impressive list of authors and editors in the What Works for Special-Needs Learners series. It's a real honor. We also appreciate their incredible patience, as it took us much longer than anticipated to produce the manuscript.

We thank our stellar lineup of authors for sharing their insights, talents, and time with us—and for producing such stimulating and informative chapters. Special thanks to CAST's Communications Director, David Gordon, for helping shape the book from concept to final product and for bringing two decades of editorial wisdom and expertise to the process. Thanks also to Research Associate Scott Lapinski for his editorial and research support. Finally, we thank Ada Sullivan, President of CAST, and all of our colleagues for giving us the time and space to complete this book, even when it might have distracted us from our day-to-day work with them. Their support was invaluable.

Contents

CHAPTER 1

An Introduction to
Universal Design for Learning

Questions and Answers

TRACEY E. HALL, ANNE MEYER, and DAVID H. ROSE

What is Universal Design for Learning, or UDL? If you're a recent graduate of an education program, you have probably heard the term in your preservice courses. If you're a practicing educator, you may have read about UDL in a professional journal, or attended a workshop in which UDL was the topic or was mentioned as a framework for planning. You may know that federal education law provides for incorporating UDL into teacher training (both preservice and inservice). You may have heard that UDL has something to do with technology, personalized learning, neuroscience, or differentiated instruction. Regardless of what you have heard or read, you may want to know more, and that's why you've picked up this book.

In this chapter, we answer that primary question—"What is UDL?"—along with many others you may have. In doing so, we aim to provide you with a good grasp of the fundamentals of UDL. In subsequent chapters, you will read about how UDL is put into practice at different grade levels and across varying content areas. Those chapters will be even more helpful to you once you read this overview. And if you want to know more, we invite you to visit our websites (*http://www.cast.org* and *http://www.udlcenter.org*).

WHAT IS UDL?

UDL is a framework for instruction organized around three principles based on the learning sciences. These principles guide the design and development of curriculum that is effective and inclusive for all learners (Rose & Gravel, 2010).

Based on two decades of research into the nature of learning differences and the design of supportive learning environment, the UDL principles map onto three groups of brain networks—recognition, strategic, and affective networks—that play a primary role in learning (see the next question for more on this). These are the three UDL principles (Rose & Meyer, 2002):

I. To support recognition learning, provide multiple means of representation—that is, offer flexible ways to present *what* we teach and learn.
II. To support strategic learning, provide multiple means of action and expression—that is, flexible options for *how* we learn and express what we know.
III. To support affective learning, provide multiple means of engagement—that is, flexible options for generating and sustaining motivation, the *why* of learning.

In the Higher Education Opportunity Act (HEOA; Public Law 110-315, August 14, 2008), Congress defines UDL as

a scientifically valid framework for guiding educational practice that—

(A) provides flexibility in the ways information is presented, in the ways students respond or demonstrate knowledge and skills, and in the ways students are engaged; and
(B) reduces barriers in instruction, provides appropriate accommodations, supports, and challenges, and maintains high achievement expectations for all students, including students with disabilities and students who are limited English proficient.

For more on how the UDL principles are applied in practice, see Lapinski, Gravel, and Rose's discussion of the UDL Guidelines version 2.0 (CAST, 2011) in Chapter 2, as well as other chapters in this book.

WHAT ARE THE THREE GROUPS OF BRAIN NETWORKS?

Advances in neuroscience and education research over the past 40 years have reshaped our understanding of the learning brain. One of the clearest and most important revelations stemming from brain research is that there is no such thing as a "regular student." Instead, learning is as unique to individuals as their fingerprints or DNA. The notion of broad categories of learners—"smart–not smart," "disabled–not disabled," "regular–not regular"—is a gross oversimplification that does not reflect reality. By categorizing students in this way, we miss many subtle and important qualities and strengths. Science shows that individual qualities or abilities are not static and fixed; rather, they are continually shifting, and they exist in relationship to the environment. The intersection between the individual and the environment is a dynamic and complex balancing act. In short, there is tremendous variability among individuals in how they perceive and interact with any environment, including the classroom. Variability and difference, therefore, constitute the *norm* from student to student—even among those who seem to share similar characteristics, such as culture, age, race, or level of success. The differences among the "A students" in any given class are as stark as those among the "A students" and "F students."

This reframes our understanding of learners away from the vision of education based on the needs of some mythical "average" learner who can be counted on to experience a curriculum in a certain "average" way. We know that variability is the rule, both within and among all individuals, and that such variability is systematic rather than random.

At CAST (an educational nonprofit organization focused on promoting and researching UDL), we refer to three sets of brain networks that, taken together, can help us better understand how the brain functions during learning episodes. This is simply a model—a fairly basic way to partition the learning brain. There are other, more complex models of brain activity that address many different networks or functions. But this model reveals the fundamental foundations of learning, and it enables us to analyze the curriculum and how learners interact with it. The three groups of networks are as follows:

- "Recognition networks" are specialized to sense and assign meaning to patterns we see; they enable us to identify and understand information, ideas, and concepts. This is the "what" of learning.
- "Strategic networks" relate primarily to the executive functions and are specialized to generate and oversee mental and motor patterns. They enable us to plan, execute, and monitor actions and skills. This is the "how" of learning.
- "Affective networks" are specialized to evaluate patterns and assign them emotional significance; they enable us to engage with tasks and learning and with the world around us. This is the "why" of learning.

These three sets of neural networks, though distinguishable, work closely together to coordinate even simple acts. For example, say you want to wrap a present for a friend. Recognition networks enable you to identify the present, the wrap, and the concept of a gift. Strategic networks help you set your goal of wrapping the present and make a strategy for accomplishing this; they guide you through the folding and taping, allow you to monitor your progress, and permit you to make small adjustments (such as refolding a corner) until the task is complete. Affective networks motivate you to take on this task as you think about your friend, and they help you persist through the various steps, keeping you on task; wrapping may be hard for you, but you sense how happy it will make your friend and yourself, so you persist.

Understanding the recognition, strategic, and affective networks and their interrelations can help us appreciate the differences each individual brings to the learning process—and the need for flexibility in the "what," "how," and "why" of learning.

WHY IS UDL NECESSARY?

The principles of UDL enable us to recognize that variance across individuals is the *norm*, not the exception, wherever people are gathered. Therefore, the curriculum should be adaptable to individual differences rather than the other way around. In this sense, traditional curricula have the "disability," because they only work for certain learners. They are filled with barriers that are erected at the point of curriculum design, especially when printed text is the near-exclusive medium. Learners with disabilities are the most vulnerable to such barriers: Those with motor disabilities cannot turn pages, while individuals with dyslexia may struggle to decode the text. But many students without disabilities also find that curricula are not adequately designed to meet their learning needs.

As standards-based reform movements have arisen and gained strength over the past quarter-century, federal, state, and local education agencies have placed increasing emphasis on providing all individuals with equal opportunities to learn in the general education curriculum. This has changed the makeup of classrooms dramatically, as students with disabilities and students with various cultural and linguistic backgrounds are included in general education settings and expected to succeed. Furthermore, the cost of retrofitting inaccessible materials has led to a rethinking of how curriculum is designed and delivered.

The challenge for teachers can be daunting. Although teachers do not want their students to fail, many feel that they lack a guiding framework—one allowing for instructional design that is inclusive of the vast linguistic, cultural, and cognitive variability present within their classrooms each year. UDL provides us with such a framework.

SO IS UDL SPECIAL EDUCATION OR GENERAL EDUCATION?

UDL encompasses education for all learners, which of course includes general and special education, early education and postsecondary education. In fact, UDL enables us to envision a time when there will be one curriculum that is designed to be truly appropriate for all learners. "Universal" doesn't mean "one-size-fits-all." Rather, it means that all learners with all their individual differences have equal and fair access and opportunity to learn the same content in ways that work best for them.

We recognize that under the current system there is a need for special education. Indeed, the development of special education was a critical step forward for students with disabilities, because it guaranteed them an education that they were once shut out of completely.

However, experience tells us that separate is seldom equal, and the idea of separating students with certain differences from their peers suggests that the "disability" resides in those individuals, not in the curriculum itself. As general education becomes more flexible through UDL, it should be able to serve the needs and interests of all learners.

WHAT IS UDL'S RELATIONSHIP TO UNIVERSAL DESIGN?

The term "Universal Design for Learning" (UDL) echoes a concept from architecture and product development called "universal design (UD)." What makes UDL different is its focus on *learning*. The principles central to UDL reflect that focus: They address the dynamic processes of teaching and learning.

Originally formulated by Ron Mace at North Carolina State University, UD supports the development of buildings, outdoor spaces, products, and communications that meet the needs of individuals with disabilities at the design stage. This practice has spread to such areas as civic engineering and commercial product design. Designs that from the start increase accessibility for individuals with disabilities tend to yield benefits that make everyone's experiences better.

The development of closed captioning on television provides a good example of UD in practice. When captioning first became available, it was intended for people with hearing impairments. However, it now benefits not only those with hearing impairments, but also exercisers in health clubs, travelers in airports, and individuals working on their language skills.

UDL shares a goal with UD—considering as many individuals as possible with designs that work from the outset and do not require retrofitting. However, the principles and techniques for accomplishing this are quite different in education, since creating learning experiences is a fundamentally different process from building things (Rose & Meyer, 2002, 2005).

WHAT IS THE RESEARCH BASIS FOR UDL?

For its work on UDL, CAST has drawn on research from several sources. First, research from neuroscience forms the basis for the UDL principles. In recent years, new technologies have allowed researchers to investigate the neurology of learning in ways that were unimaginable even a decade ago. This research has produced two findings that are critical to UDL: (1) Learning in the individual brain is highly diverse and distributed, and (2) learning *among* different individuals is also highly diverse and distributed. The foundational research in cognitive neuroscience, cognitive science, and other learning sciences is critical in articulating the range of what learning is, and what the range of individual differences in learning are. When learning is considered too narrowly, then we are likely to create curricula and lessons that are too poorly differentiated to optimize learning.

Second, CAST's work on UDL draws from research identifying the specific practices that are critical to supporting all students—research that has been amassed over decades and by many different researchers in many universities and laboratories. Typically these practices have already proven effective for individual students "in the margins," but they are generally not integrated within the standard "one-size-fits-all" curriculum of general education. UDL provides a vehicle for delivering these practices to the individual students for whom they are likely to be most effective. But which practices, and for whom? The UDL approach offers both a framework and guidelines to help in making informed decisions about what practices are optimal. The purpose of the framework is to ensure comprehensiveness, and to ensure that the instructional designs will address the full range of learning abilities and disabilities present in any group of students. See Chapter 2 for more specifics on how the UDL is applied to curriculum development.

Third, CAST has utilized the research on specific applications of UDL. This kind of research is nascent (since UDL itself was articulated less than two decades ago), but exemplars are emerging. For example, researchers at CAST have developed and evaluated an illustration of UDL as it is applied to the teaching of reading comprehension strategies. Chapter 3 provides more details about this work. Other chapters in this book also discuss research on specific implementations.

WHAT DOES IT MEAN TO SAY THAT UDL APPLIES TO THE WHOLE CURRICULUM?

We see any curriculum as having four essential components—goals, assessments, materials, and methods—and each should be designed with consideration for all learners (Rose & Meyer, 2002). In each of this book's chapters, the authors address these fundamental components in light of the UDL principles and particular content areas (science, math, history, etc.).

Goals need to be clearly defined so that they provide appropriate challenges for all learners—and don't raise unintentional barriers in how they are articulated. For example, if a goal is to learn the stages of photosynthesis, the statement of that goal should not prescribe the methods and materials for accomplishing it (e.g., "Read a chapter about photosynthesis"), since some otherwise capable learners may not be able to use those particular methods and materials.

Assessments, both during (formative) and following (summative) learning episodes, need to be sufficiently flexible (1) to provide accurate information on how well learners are meeting goals, and (2) to inform adjustments in methods and materials to make instruction more effective. Assessments can and should be designed to provide assessment data to guide not only overall instructional activities for the classroom, but also just-in-time adjustments for individual students.

Instructional methods and materials should be flexible and varied to provide the right balance of access, challenge, and support for learners, and to allow learners to achieve their goals in the ways that work best for each individual.

WHY ARE TECHNOLOGY AND UDL SO OFTEN DISCUSSED TOGETHER?

Many classrooms continue to be dominated by a single, inflexible medium—printed textbooks. We categorize as "disabled" those students for whom a printed textbook is difficult or impossible to use. We then prescribe for them special goals, teaching methods, and materials, often with a remedial focus. Even students able to access text are missing out, because we know that there are other media more suitable for communicating particular kinds of material, and for deepening particular students' engagement with that material.

UDL, on the other hand, calls for taking advantage of the power and customizability of modern technology to deliver, by design, flexible instructional practices directly within the core instructional curriculum where students can access them on an individualized basis. These best practices, often essential for students identified with disabilities or other struggling learners, often prove advantageous for many other students as well.

Digital media are powerful because they are versatile and transformable. Unlike a printed book, digital media can display content in many formats—text, still images, sound, moving images, or any combination of these—with just a few keystrokes. Learners visiting the same website can alter how content is presented. They can change the appearance of text or images, turn off graphics, or turn on sound. Using a program with text-to-speech capabilities, a teacher can set up a computer to read words aloud on demand for a student with dyslexia, transforming the medium from print to sound.

Digital media are also powerful because they can be networked. This makes it possible to link one piece of digital content to others via hyperlinks. For example, a digital text of the Gettysburg Address can provide embedded learning supports, such as a glossary or background-knowledge briefs, to support readers without taking them off task. (See *http://udleditions.cast.org* for an example.)

With a better understanding of new and traditional media and of how individual brains interact with each, teachers can reevaluate how they teach, how students learn, and how best to use various tools and techniques to individualize these processes. The digital capacity to combine and transform text, speech, and images opens new vistas of learning for many individuals who struggle in print-only environments (Rose & Meyer, 2002, 2005; Rose & Gravel, 2009).

CAN THE UDL PRINCIPLES BE APPLIED WITHOUT TECHNOLOGY?

Although technology can be an important factor in implementing UDL, it is not a requirement. It is understood that many schools have outdated computers, poor software, or insufficient access to computer labs for teachers to take advantage of technology in implementing their curricula. While this divide between applicability and access can surely be a source of frustration, excellent UDL instruction can be achieved without technology, and many examples of such instruction are described throughout this book. For example, Chapter 9 discusses an elementary school lesson where the goal is to help students understand and be able to articulate their understanding of the life cycle of plants. Even though it does not use technology, it can still be considered UDL. There certainly might be ways that technology could be beneficial in this lesson, but it is not essential.

*   *   *

By embracing UDL both in principle and in practice, we can dramatically improve learning opportunities for all learners. UDL provides a blueprint for designing curricula that accommodate learner differences. Chapter 2 presents the UDL Guidelines; it is followed by chapters focused on specific content areas: reading, writing, mathematics, science, history, and the arts. In these chapters, the authors discuss the challenges of teaching these subjects given the tremendous variability of individual learners as documented by neuroscience, as well as the diversity of learners as measured by educational experiences, cultural backgrounds, and disability. The authors then demonstrate some of the common barriers to learning and suggest ways to design more inclusive learning environments. Technology plays an especially supportive role in most cases, but the authors also show how UDL can be applied in low-tech or no-tech ways. Chapter 9 addresses UDL in a no-tech environment (specifically, an elementary-grade classroom) head on, offering helpful insights from practice. Rounding out the book is Chapter 10's discussion of UDL in postsecondary settings, where preservice instructors can not only learn about but also experience UDL. In assembling this book, we aim to provide a helpful introduction to UDL. We hope that you, the reader, will view this not as a prescription but as an invitation: We invite you to join the conversation and to share your wisdom with others. Visit *http://www.udlcenter.org* to find a community of educators who together are exploring ways to reform education in positive ways at the point of curriculum design and implementation, with the UDL principles as their guide.

REFERENCES

CAST. (2011). *Universal Design for Learning Guidelines version 2.0.* Wakefield, MA: Author. Retrieved from *http://www.udlcenter.org/aboutudl/udlguidelines.*

Higher Education Opportunity Act (HEOA). (2008, August 14). Public Law 110-315. Retrieved from *http://www2.ed.gov/policy/highered/leg/hea08/index.html.*

Rose, D. H., & Gravel, J. W. (2009). Getting from here to there: UDL, global positioning systems, and lessons for improving education. In D. T. Gordon, J. W. Gravel, & L. A. Schifter (Eds.), *A policy reader in Universal Design for Learning* (pp. 5–18) Cambridge, MA: Harvard Education Press.

Rose, D. H., & Gravel, J. W. (2010). Universal Design for Learning. In P. Peterson, E. Baker, & B. McGraw (Eds.), *International encyclopedia of education* (pp. 119–124). Oxford, UK: Elsevier.

Rose, D. H., & Meyer, A. (2002). *Teaching every student in the digital age: Universal Design for Learning.* Alexandria, VA: Association for Supervision and Curriculum Development.

Rose, D. H., & Meyer, A. (Eds.). (2005). *A practical reader in Universal Design for Learning.* Cambridge, MA: Harvard Education Press.

CHAPTER 2

Tools for Practice

The Universal Design for Learning Guidelines

SCOTT LAPINSKI, JENNA W. GRAVEL, and DAVID H. ROSE

This book is written to provide classroom teachers with fresh insights on how technology can be used to extend learning opportunities to all students, including those "in the margins" (Meyer & Rose, 2005). In particular, the chapter authors focus on the use of technology in learning environments that emphasize the principles of Universal Design for Learning (UDL). The authors refer specifically and more generally to the principles, guidelines, and checkpoints that are at the heart of UDL implementation. This chapter offers an overview of the UDL Guidelines version 2.0 (CAST, 2011), which constitute a practical articulation of the broader UDL principles discussed by Hall, Meyer, and Rose in Chapter 1. They allow us to see how we might carefully plan and structure curricular goals, methods, materials, and assessments to ensure that barriers to student learning are removed. They are based on a wealth of research in the learning sciences and educational practice; visit the National Center on Universal Design for Learning (*http://www.udlcenter.org*) for a detailed list of references.

PURPOSES OF THIS CHAPTER

In this chapter, we have three different purposes. First we address what the UDL Guidelines are and why they were created. Then we discuss the specific content of the Guidelines, walking through the three levels of organization: principles → Guidelines → checkpoints. Finally, we discuss who might use the Guidelines and how they might be implemented to reduce barriers and maximize opportunities for all learners. Subsequent chapters in this volume discuss specific applications of the Guidelines to particular content areas and grade levels.

After reading this chapter, you should be able to answer two questions: What are the UDL Guidelines? And how might you (a teacher, curriculum developer, parent, etc.) use the Guidelines?

WHAT ARE THE UDL GUIDELINES?

The UDL Guidelines are tools to help teachers and other curriculum developers in the instructional planning stage (Meo, 2008). As their name suggests, they are meant to provide guidance, not prescriptions, for inclusive classroom practice. Teachers can use the Guidelines to gain a sense of the options that they can build into their curricula in order to ensure that all students are learning. They offer some potential solutions to address the barriers that many students encounter in today's classrooms.

How learning occurs varies for every individual. In particular, all learners differ greatly in "what" they learn, "how" they learn, and "why" they learn (Coyne et al., 2006; Rose & Meyer, 2002). Research from neuroscience has helped us to understand that even students who appear to be similar are actually quite different. Since no two students are the same, the whole curriculum—the goals, methods, materials, and assessments—must capably address the strengths and weaknesses of individual students as they move collectively toward achieving high academic standards.

The UDL Guidelines support the important process of customizing instruction for individuals. They help incorporate appropriate and adjustable supports, scaffolds, and challenges into the instructional environment from the very beginning, rather than making changes or modifications as afterthoughts or add-ons. The goal in designing a UDL environment is to create lessons and/or curricula that are accessible to all students through careful planning and design. Notice the emphasis on customizable *supports* and *challenges*. Balancing supports and challenges is an important part of the UDL framework. The point here is not to make learning easier; instead, learning should be challenging—filled with what have been called "desirable difficulties" (Bjork & Bjork, 2011). The aim of UDL is to maintain those desirable difficulties while reducing or eliminating "undesirable difficulties," barriers to learning that arise and that are irrelevant to the goals of learning.

Applying the UDL Guidelines has been compared to using a Global Positioning System (GPS) device (Rose & Gravel, 2009; see also *http://www.udlcenter.org/resource_library/articles/gps*). A GPS device offers a range of embedded options to account for the diversity among individuals and asks three central questions in order to customize to users' preferences: "What is your present location? What is your destination or goal? What is the best route for reaching that goal?" (Rose & Gravel, 2009, p. 5). A GPS device is a useful analogy with which to illustrate the UDL Guidelines, because these three questions are so critical when we think about student learning. As educators, we must address these same questions as we are planning, delivering, and reflecting upon our lessons in order to reach the diverse learners in our classrooms.

THE UDL GUIDELINES AND THE THREE UDL PRINCIPLES

The UDL Guidelines were developed in response to calls from the education field for practical advice in how to implement the three UDL principles. The framework of UDL approaches the challenge of learning differences from a new perspective: We shift the emphasis from retrofitting a one-size-fits-all curriculum to designing a more flexible curriculum that works for all students from the start. In traditional settings, we tend to label as "disabled" or "underachieving" those individuals whom the curriculum fails, which results in trying to "fix" these students. Instead, the UDL approach focuses on curricular "disabilities," because it is the curriculum that cannot meet the learning needs of all students and needs to be fixed.

In daily practice, we unintentionally build barriers by the way we design our instruction, and this can occur in any part of the curriculum (goals, methods, materials, and assessments). For example, requiring students to express their knowledge by writing a five-paragraph essay will automatically limit how students can express their knowledge. If expressing what they know is the goal, why impose the limited medium of the written essay? In such a situation, students who have motor difficulties, students who are English language learners (ELLs), or students who have weaknesses in organization, for example, may not be able to accurately express what they know despite the fact that they understand the content. (If demonstrating skill in essay writing *is* the goal, then that's a different story; other options can be embedded into the lesson to support skills that do not infringe upon the writing goal.) Fortunately even a brief introduction to UDL can be beneficial in planning lessons that include all students (Schelly, Davies, & Spooner, 2011).

The UDL Guidelines are organized around the three principles of UDL: (I) Provide multiple means of representation; (II) provide multiple means of action and expression; and (III) provide multiple means of engagement (Rose & Gravel, 2010). The Guidelines and checkpoints are listed under each principle to provide educators and curriculum developers with a sense of potential barriers and solutions in curriculum design and implementation. Visit the National Center on UDL (*http://www.udlcenter.org/aboutudl/udlguidelines*) for the complete research, examples, and resources supporting the Guidelines.

THE GUIDELINES AND TECHNOLOGY

What role does technology play in applying the UDL Guidelines? Technology gives us many opportunities to customize education to meet individual needs. We are able to provide students with digital texts that offer a range of embedded supports and scaffolds (e.g., text-to-speech [TTS] capabilities, links to background information, glossaries). We can offer a range of expressive tools from which students can choose to convey what they have learned (e.g., PowerPoint, animation software, graphic organizers, voice recognition software). We can even connect and communicate with students and classrooms around the world through online collaboration tools and blogs. Technology helps make learning possible for many different students by creating flexible and supportive learning environments from the beginning of instruction (Strangman & Dalton, 2005), and you will find numerous examples of this throughout this book.

Yet even in low-tech or no-tech classrooms, the Guidelines are applicable (for an example, see Rose, Gravel, & Domings, Chapter 9, this volume). The power and flexibility of modern technology may make it easier to implement UDL, but technology is not central to the UDL framework. The Guidelines are a set of suggestions that can be considered when planning instruction with or without technology, but there is an important exception. The Guidelines remind us:

> For some students, the use of personal assistive technologies—e.g., an electric wheelchair, eyeglasses, or a cochlear implant—is essential for basic physical and sensory access to learning environments. Those students will need their assistive technologies, even during activities where other students may not use any technologies at all. Even in classrooms that are well equipped with UDL materials and methods, their assistive technology neither precludes nor replaces the need for UDL overall. (CAST, 2011, p. 10)

For students who require assistive technology, such technology represents an essential component to learning and cannot be dismissed. Yet, in general, the Guidelines offer educators tools for creating flexible, inclusive environments that foster learning for all students, be it online or offline.

APPLYING THE GUIDELINES: RATIONALES AND SPECIFIC EXAMPLES

How are the UDL Guidelines applied to curriculum development? Figure 2.1 offers a handy overview of the three UDL principles, the UDL Guidelines, and their associated checkpoints. In the following pages, we explain the rationales for the Guidelines and provide even more specific examples of what they might look like in practice. In implementing the Guidelines, it is important to remember that all three principles are equally valuable. Disregarding a principle might create unintentional barriers for learners, and therefore all three should be carefully considered.

Principle I: Provide Multiple Means of Representation

The first principle of UDL (highlighted in Figure 2.2) is all about the "what" of learning. By "what," we mean how information is perceived and comprehended. Individuals perceive and comprehend information in many different ways, so no

I. Provide Multiple Means of Representation

1: Provide options for perception
1.1 Offer ways of customizing the display of information
1.2 Offer alternatives for auditory information
1.3 Offer alternatives for visual information

2: Provide options for language, mathematical expressions, and symbols
2.1 Clarify vocabulary and symbols
2.2 Clarify syntax and structure
2.3 Support decoding of text, mathematical notation, and symbols
2.4 Promote understanding across languages
2.5 Illustrate through multiple media

3: Provide options for comprehension
3.1 Activate or supply background knowledge
3.2 Highlight patterns, critical features, big ideas, and relationships
3.3 Guide information processing, visualization, and manipulation
3.4 Maximize transfer and generalization

Resourceful, knowledgeable learners

II. Provide Multiple Means of Action and Expression

4: Provide options for physical action
4.1 Vary the methods for response and navigation
4.2 Optimize access to tools and assistive technologies

5: Provide options for expression and communication
5.1 Use multiple media for communication
5.2 Use multiple tools for construction and composition
5.3 Build fluencies with graduated levels of support for practice and performance

6: Provide options for executive functions
6.1 Guide appropriate goal-setting
6.2 Support planning and strategy development
6.3 Facilitate managing information and resources
6.4 Enhance capacity for monitoring progress

Strategic, goal-directed learners

III. Provide Multiple Means of Engagement

7: Provide options for recruiting interest
7.1 Optimize individual choice and autonomy
7.2 Optimize relevance, value, and authenticity
7.3 Minimize threats and distractions

8: Provide options for sustaining effort and persistence
8.1 Heighten salience of goals and objectives
8.2 Vary demands and resources to optimize challenge
8.3 Foster collaboration and community
8.4 Increase mastery-oriented feedback

9: Provide options for self-regulation
9.1 Promote expectations and beliefs that optimize motivation
9.2 Facilitate personal coping skills and strategies
9.3 Develop self-assessment and reflection

Purposeful, motivated learners

FIGURE 2.1. The UDL Guidelines. Copyright 2011 by CAST, Inc. All rights reserved. Used with permission.

one medium of representation is going to serve the needs of all learners or even of an individual learner. For some, text is challenging, especially in the inflexible medium of print, while others may struggle to understand an audio track without a transcript. There are also differences in comprehension; each student brings a unique set of personal experiences and background knowledge. Since there is such a wide range of individual differences in representation, there is no one right way to present or make available what we want students to learn. The curriculum should have enough flexibility for students and teachers to determine the most appropriate way to access the content.

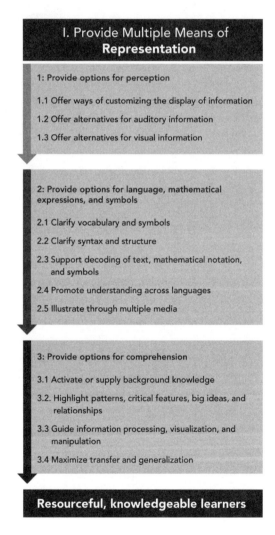

FIGURE 2.2. The UDL Guidelines: Principle I highlighted. Copyright 2011 by CAST, Inc. All rights reserved. Used with permission.

Guideline 1: Provide Options for Perception

Guideline 1 reminds us that it is critical to provide options in the ways that students perceive information. It can be thought of more as an "access" guideline, as it focuses on providing students with ways into the content. Unintended barriers arise when information is not presented through various media. For example, providing students with information presented only in text will automatically create a barrier to students who are struggling readers or to students who have visual impairments. Options such as TTS software, graphics, videos, and other presentation formats can be effective alternatives. Similarly, if information is only given in an audio format, then some students will not have access. A lecture, for example, may pose a barrier, as the pace may be too fast or a student may not be able to hear clearly. The point is this: Presenting information in only one way will unnecessarily exclude some students from the curriculum.

Guideline 2: Provide Options for Language, Mathematical Expressions, and Symbols

Providing options for perception may not address all of the potential barriers associated with representation of content. Guideline 2 prompts us to consider providing options for language, mathematical expressions, and symbols. The students in our classes have a broad range of strengths and challenges with various forms of representations. If we present information through a single language, students with decoding difficulties, students with dyslexia, or students who are ELLs, for example, will not have access to content. For this reason, it is important to incorporate such strategies as preteaching important terms, providing multimedia glossaries, offering alternative languages and translation supports, and utilizing images and video in order to help make academic content more accessible.

Our system of symbols raises similar concerns. As an example, mathematics is essentially a language of its own, and it is a language that some students struggle with (Geary, 2004; see also Murray & Brookover, Chapter 6, this volume). A possible option to help such students is to use manipulatives to make the symbols more concrete (Murray, Silver-Pacuilla, & Helsel, 2007). For example, when developing young students' understanding of the division symbol, a teacher can represent the division process by having students break apart a group of interlocking blocks into equal groups. This alternative representation allows students to interact with the mathematical concept of division in a way that might be impossible if only the symbol was used. Similar strategies can be applied to the sciences (see Price, Johnson, & Barnett, Chapter 5, this volume), as well as to other specialty content areas.

Guideline 3: Provide Options for Comprehension

Guideline 3 prompts us to provide options for comprehension. Even the best presentation is not effective if students are not able to process the information; students need to *understand* the information that is being presented to them. Guideline 3 reminds us that knowledge is created when students are actively engaged, not passively absorbing, and that not all students can accomplish this independently. For this reason, the checkpoints for Guideline 3 stress the importance of activating or supplying background knowledge; providing students with models and scaffolds to highlight critical features, big ideas, and relationships; to guide information processing, visualization, and manipulation; and to facilitate the transfer and generalization of knowledge to different contexts (e.g., see Gordon, Proctor, & Dalton, Chapters 3, and Robinson & Meyer, Chapter 7, this volume).

Principle II: Provide Multiple Means of Action and Expression

Learning involves more than acquiring information; it is also a proactive and expressive endeavor, requiring skills in strategy, organization, and communication. And again, the way in which individuals approach learning tasks and express their understanding may differ dramatically from person to person. In short, the second principle of UDL (highlighted in Figure 2.3) addresses the "how" of learning. Typically, educators/teachers ask students to produce text (write) or present (orally state) what they understand through questioning, activities and assessments. When we apply this principle of UDL concerning action and expression, we can apply additional options and avenues for how students demonstrate their knowledge in the learning process.

Guideline 4: Provide Options for Physical Action

As Guideline 1 does, Guideline 4 addresses overtly physical barriers. In this case, it encourages us to consider options for physical action so that students' motor skills do not hinder expression. For example, traditional curricula usually call for either writing or orally responding—such as writing by hand in a workbook, answering out loud, or using a word processor. Those means may not be accessible to some learners who have weaknesses in motor skills, who have blindness/low vision, or who have severe dyslexia. In order to overcome these barriers, Guideline 4 suggests providing multiple means of response. This is where expressive options such as audio recording, voice recognition software, alternative keyboards or joysticks, and other forms of assistive technology come into play.

Guideline 5: Provide Options for Expression and Communication

Guideline 5 helps us to focus on providing options for how students approach learning tasks and how they express themselves. Learners vary in terms of how they can communicate and how they best solve problems. In addition, they may need models of skilled performance and ample time for practice, with scaffolds that can be gradually released. Guideline 5 also reminds us that building fluency in a skill—that is, the rate at which a person can perform an activity—is essential. The

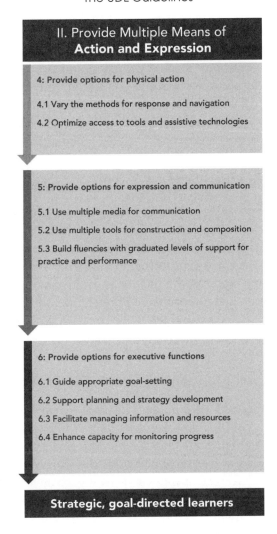

II. Provide Multiple Means of Action and Expression

4: Provide options for physical action

4.1 Vary the methods for response and navigation

4.2 Optimize access to tools and assistive technologies

5: Provide options for expression and communication

5.1 Use multiple media for communication

5.2 Use multiple tools for construction and composition

5.3 Build fluencies with graduated levels of support for practice and performance

6: Provide options for executive functions

6.1 Guide appropriate goal-setting

6.2 Support planning and strategy development

6.3 Facilitate managing information and resources

6.4 Enhance capacity for monitoring progress

Strategic, goal-directed learners

FIGURE 2.3. The UDL Guidelines: Principle II highlighted. Copyright 2011 by CAST, Inc. All rights reserved. Used with permission.

most obvious example is in reading. A student who reads fluently will have a better chance at comprehending the material, because he or she is not weighted down with decoding individual words. Fluency is something that must be practiced and taught, and students need options for how and when to build automaticity.

Guideline 6: Provide Options for Executive Functions

Think of what business executives do. They excel at setting goals, making plans and strategies, organizing, and monitoring progress. They set reachable, short-term goals, but can simultaneously work toward broader, long-term goals. These skills are crucial to learning as well, and Guideline 6 reminds us of the importance of scaffolding students' executive functions. We can help students develop critical thinking skills by providing such options as guides to develop goal setting, checklists to support planning, and models to encourage effective note taking. Furthermore, it is important to prompt students to "stop and think" about the work that they are doing. As educators, we want to continually monitor students' progress and help students to develop the skills to monitor *their own* progress at the same time. In short, providing options for executive functions is essential for students to become independent, expert learners.

Principle III: Provide Multiple Means of Engagement

What motivates students to learn? What makes them persist even when tasks are hard or boring? How can they self-regulate their own learning, the way effective lifelong learners must? The answers vary from person to person. Some students work best when they have a strict routine, while others like to be more spontaneous. Some students are most productive, or learn best with specific goals, while others need a more open-ended approach. Three guidelines address and articulate the third principle of UDL (highlighted in Figure 2.4), which covers the "why" of learning.

Guideline 7: Provide Options for Recruiting Interest

If students are not interested, they are less likely to learn. There are many ways to recruit student interest, but the research tells us that one of the best ways to pique our students' interest is to provide choice, although types and levels of choice will both vary. Students need to feel responsible for the work they are doing—to have a sense of "ownership." To recruit interest, learning goals and activities must also seem valuable and relevant to the learners. One successful approach is to ensure that activities are as authentic as possible, thus increasing interest, providing a sense of purpose, and (ideally) making it easier for students to connect the information to their background knowledge. Of course, for this to occur, students must feel safe within the learning environment. Teachers and students can work together to reduce threats and distractions, and to build a classroom community that is appreciative, supportive, challenging, and inclusive.

Guideline 8: Provide Options for Sustaining Effort and Persistence

Guideline 8 reminds us that students need options that appropriately balance challenge and support in order to ensure that learning occurs most efficiently. If the activity is too difficult, students will get frustrated; if it's too easy, they may become bored. The challenge–support balance can be found by creating opportunities to collaborate with peers or by providing alternatives in the tools and scaffolds offered for a particular assignment. Finally, it is important to provide students with feedback that allows them to see that practice and persistence are most important for

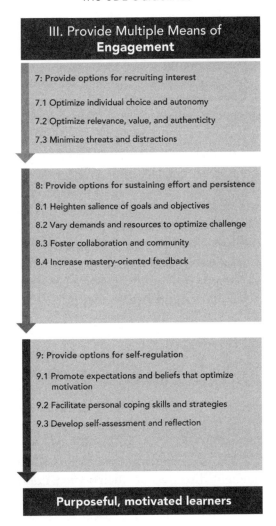

FIGURE 2.4. The UDL Guidelines: Principle III highlighted. Copyright 2011 by CAST, Inc. All rights reserved. Used with permission.

success. Without feedback, learners won't know what they can improve upon and what they are doing well.

Guideline 9: Provide Options for Self-Regulation

In many cases, Guideline 9 gets the least attention in practice, because it represents a shift from the external environment to the students' internal environment. However, this should not be the case: To create lifelong learners, it is essential to support students' ability to regulate their own learning. Students need to develop the skills to set appropriate personal goals and the strategies to cope with their own emotions. They also need the ability to assess their own progress and to reflect upon their individual strengths and weaknesses as learners. Guideline 9 thus prompts us to consider implementing strategies into our practice to develop students' intrinsic abilities to regulate their own emotions and motivations.

HOW DO YOU USE THE GUIDELINES?

Like UDL itself, the UDL Guidelines are flexible; they should be mixed and matched in the curriculum and with individual learners as appropriate. The UDL Guidelines are not meant to be "prescriptions" but strategies that can be employed to overcome the barriers inherent in most existing curricula. While it is true that educators may find an array of individual uses for the Guidelines, they can be most useful for three main purposes: as tools to support the design of lessons or units; as tools to assess instructional methods or materials; and as tools for facilitating discussion about the curriculum. No matter what the teaching strategy, teachers must engage in careful planning, and this is where the Guidelines become critical.

Tools for Lesson/Unit Development

The Guidelines are effective tools for individual educators or for teams of educators who are designing lessons or unit plans. Instead of making time-consuming accommodations or modifications to lessons according to individual students' needs, the Guidelines can support the development of lessons that consider the broadest range of learners from the outset. The UDL Guidelines and associated checkpoints prompt educators to consider ways to design multiple means of representation, action/expression, and engagement directly into their instruction. Figure 2.1 shows the Guidelines and checkpoints for each UDL principle; many teachers have found this one-page document helpful in their planning, because it serves as a visual reminder of the different options that they can consider when designing lessons to meet the needs of all of their students. In addition, the UDL Guidelines—Educator Checklist (Figure 2.5) helps practitioners consider specific Guidelines or checkpoints and then make notes on how they might embed these strategies into their lessons.

It is important to reiterate that the UDL Guidelines should be applied according to the specific goals of each lesson or unit. It is not necessary, or even advisable, to incorporate all of the Guidelines into every lesson. For example, a teacher who is designing a lesson around effective essay writing would not want to apply Guideline 5, which suggests providing *options* in the media for communication. If the goal of the lesson is writing an essay, students should not be offered the choice to express their ideas through different media, such as through a poster, a video, or a 3-D model. However, the teacher could consider other Guidelines that would support the objective of this lesson. Perhaps he or she may want to scaffold students' executive functions (Guideline 6) and provide a graphic organizer or a template to support the organization of students' ideas. Or, as a way to recruit students' interest

I. Provide Multiple Means of Representation:	Your notes
1. Provide options for perception	
1.1 Offer ways of customizing the display of information	
1.2 Offer alternatives for auditory information	
1.3 Offer alternatives for visual information	
2. Provide options for language, mathematical expressions, and symbols	
2.1 Clarify vocabulary and symbols	
2.2 Clarify syntax and structure	
2.3 Support decoding of text, mathematical notation, and symbols	
2.4 Promote understanding across language	
2.5 Illustrate through multiple media	
3. Provide options for comprehension	
3.1 Activate or supply background knowledge	
3.2 Highlight patterns, critical features, big ideas, and relationships	
3.3 Guide information processing, visualization, and manipulation	
3.4 Maximize transfer and generalization	
II. Provide Multiple Means for Action and Expression:	Your notes
4. Provide options for physical action	
4.1 Vary the methods for response and navigation	
4.2 Optimize access to tools and assistive technologies	
5. Provide options for expression and communication	
5.1 Use multiple media for communication	
5.2 Use multiple tools for construction and composition	
5.3 Build fluencies with graduated levels of support for practice and performance	
6. Provide options for executive functions	
6.1 Guide appropriate goal setting	
6.2 Support planning and strategy development	
6.3 Facilitate managing information and resources	
6.4 Enhance capacity for monitoring progress	
III. Provide Multiple Means for Engagement:	Your notes
7. Provide options for recruiting interest	
7.1 Optimize individual choice and autonomy	
7.2 Optimize relevance, value, and authenticity	
7.3 Minimize threats and distractions	
8. Provide options for sustaining effort and persistence	
8.1 Heighten salience of goals and objectives	
8.2 Vary demands and resources to optimize challenge	
8.3 Foster collaboration and community	
8.4 Increase mastery-oriented feedback	
9. Provide options for self-regulation	
9.1 Promote expectations and beliefs that optimize motivation	
9.2 Facilitate personal coping skills and strategies	
9.3 Develop self-assessment and reflection	

FIGURE 2.5. UDL Guidelines—Educator Checklist. Copyright 2011 by CAST, Inc. All rights reserved. Used with permission.

(Guideline 7), perhaps the teacher may want to offer a choice in essay topic. The Guidelines are a flexible set of suggestions and can be applied as the teacher deems appropriate.

Tools to Assess Instructional Methods or Materials

The UDL Guidelines can also be used as effective tools to determine whether any barriers are present in an existing curriculum. It can be a valuable exercise to use the Guidelines as a framework for reflecting upon a lesson that may have been ineffective for some students. The specific strategies suggested by the Guidelines may offer insight into ways to improve the lesson so that it reaches all learners.

CAST's UDL Online Modules offer a case story of a high school teacher who used the Guidelines as tools to assess an unsuccessful grammar unit on noun–verb agreement (*http://udlonline.cast.org/home*). The teacher was discouraged because many of her students viewed this grammar lesson as "boring" or "unimportant" and remained disengaged throughout the entire unit. She used the UDL Guidelines to reflect upon her unit and focused specifically on engagement. The teacher realized that many of her students might have been uninterested in the unit because it is so difficult for students to understand why grammar is relevant to their lives.

The teacher revised the lesson to provide a meaningful context for her students. She knew that many of them were learning to drive, and she also knew the statistics indicating that 50% of them would be involved in a motor vehicle accident within the first 2 years of receiving their licenses. Given these odds, many of her students would need to write a description of an accident in the near future. If they were to write it poorly, an insurance adjuster would be less likely to view their claim favorably. The teacher renamed the revised lesson "A Crash Course on Noun–Verb Agreement." She hoped that setting this context would make correct noun–verb agreement more relevant and meaningful to her students, thereby increasing their engagement.

Tools for Facilitating Discussion about the Curriculum

Discussions among teachers about the curriculum are constantly occurring in schools. These discussions are integral to ensuring that all students are learning and that the most effective practices are being used. One way to use the UDL Guidelines to help with this process is by using them in curriculum-planning meetings. Meeting attendees can use the Guidelines as starting points for conversations about each aspect of the curriculum: goals, methods, materials, and assessments. They can reflect upon ways to design lesson plans from the start that are more inclusive of all learners; they can also reflect upon the effectiveness of past lessons that may not have drawn from the UDL framework.

The Guidelines can also be used with more specific professional development initiatives, such as lesson study. "Lesson study" is a method for teacher reflection that was developed in Japan and has become increasingly popular in the United States. In this method, teachers collaboratively develop a research lesson, which is then taught by one teacher while the other teachers observe. After the completion of the observation, the teachers reflect on the lesson and try to come to an understanding of what works best for the lesson and for instruction in general (Lewis, 2009). As previously noted, the Guidelines can be used at the planning stage, but they can also be used to frame a discussion on the effectiveness of a lesson. Were there barriers to students' physical access to content (see Guideline 1)? Were there barriers to students' developing coping strategies and self-assessing (see Guideline 9)? Were there barriers to students' transferring their knowledge to a new situation (see Guideline 3)? Importantly, these kinds of questions help teachers reflect on their practice to figure out what works best for all students.

CONCLUSION

Many students in today's classrooms are confronted with major barriers to learning: inflexible, one-size-fits-all curricula. The UDL Guidelines offer all educators (teachers, administrators, tutors, or parents) a framework for understanding how learners vary and what types of tools and strategies they can use to help overcome unnecessary barriers. These barriers can occur across any of the three UDL principles and in any subject area. When successfully implemented, the Guidelines support teachers in their goal of developing expert learners: learners who are resourceful and knowledgeable, strategic and goal-directed, and purposeful and motivated. The remaining chapters of this book provide additional perspectives on how all learners can achieve this goal in specific contexts and content areas. The Guidelines should be considered foundational to understanding how to implement UDL across these different environments.

REFERENCES

Bjork, E. L., & Bjork, R. A. (2011). Making things hard on yourself, but in a good way: Creating desirable difficulties to enhance learning. In M. A. Gernsbacher, R. W. Pew, L. M. Hough, & J. R. Pomerantz (Eds.), *Psychology and the real world: Essays illustrating fundamental contributions to society* (pp. 56–64). New York: Worth.

CAST. (2009). *UDL Guidelines—Educator Checklist version 2.0*. Wakefield, MA: Author.

CAST. (2011). *Universal Design for Learning Guidelines version 2.0*. Wakefield, MA: Author. Retrieved from *http://www.udlcenter.org/aboutudl/udlguidelines*.

Coyne, P., Ganley, P., Hall, T.E., Meo, G., Murray, E., & Gordon, D. (2006). Applying universal design in the classroom. In D.H. Rose & A. Meyer (Eds.), *A practical reader in Universal Design for Learning* (pp. 1–13). Cambridge, MA: Harvard Education Press.

Geary, D. C. (2004). Mathematics and learning disabilities. *Journal of Learning Disabilities, 37,* 4–15.

Lewis, C. (2009). What is the nature of knowledge development in lesson study? *Educational Action Research, 17*(1), 95–110.

Meo, G. (2008). Curriculum planning for all learners: Applying Universal Design for Learning (UDL) to a high school reading comprehension program. *Preventing School Failure, 52*(2), 21–30.

Meyer, A., & Rose, D. H. (2005). The future is in the margins: The role of technology and disability in educational reform. In D. H. Rose, A. Meyer, & C. Hitchcock (Eds.), *The universally designed classroom: Accessible curriculum and digital technologies* (pp. 13–35). Cambridge, MA: Harvard Education Press.

Murray, B., Silver-Pacuilla, H., & Helsel, F. I. (2007). Improving basic mathematics instruction: Promising technology resources for students with special needs. *Technology in Action, 2*(5), 1–6, 8.

Rose, D. H., & Gravel, J. W. (2009). Getting from here to there: UDL, global positioning systems, and lessons for improving education. In D. T. Gordon, J. W. Gravel, & L. A. Schifter (Eds.), *A policy reader in Universal Design for Learning* (pp. 5–18). Cambridge, MA: Harvard Education Press.

Rose, D. H., & Gravel, J. W. (2010). Universal Design for Learning. In P. Peterson, E. Baker, & B. McGraw (Eds.), *International encyclopedia of education* (pp. 119–124). Oxford, UK: Elsevier.

Rose, D. H., & Meyer, A. (2002). *Teaching every student in the digital age: Universal Design for Learning.* Alexandria, VA: Association for Supervision and Curriculum Development.

Schelly, C. L., Davies, P. L., & Spooner, C. L. (2011). Student perceptions of faculty implementation of Universal Design for Learning. *Journal of Postsecondary Education and Disability, 24*(1), 17–30.

Strangman, N., & Dalton, B. (2005). Using technology to support struggling readers: A review of the research. In D. Edyburn, K. Higgins, & R. Boone (Eds.), *The handbook of special education technology research and practice* (pp. 545–569). Whitefish Bay, WI: Knowledge by Design.

CHAPTER 3

Reading Strategy Instruction, Universal Design for Learning, and Digital Texts

Examples of an Integrated Approach

DAVID GORDON, C. PATRICK PROCTOR, and BRIDGET DALTON

Alisha, a sixth-grade student who reads on the third-grade level, is reading a universally designed digital version of *Hatchet*, Gary Paulsen's (1999) award-winning middle school novel. Alisha and her class are participating in CAST's "Engaging the Text" project to explore the application of Universal Design for Learning (UDL) principles to make reading comprehension instruction more supportive, engaging, and effective for all learners. Wearing headphones, Alisha clicks on a read-aloud button to have the text read to her as she follows along. At the word "wilderness," she stops and clicks on the word. A definition with an image appears on screen. As she continues, the ebook prompts her to stop and think about the story, and to apply one of the reading comprehension strategies she has learned—predicting, questioning, clarifying, and summarizing.

She picks summarizing. But writing a summary is hard for Alisha; she's not sure what to do at this point. Maybe a hint would help? She clicks on a strategy hint button, and an animated "genie" pops up to offers one of several hints that are based on a rubric for good summary writing. "A good summary captures the most important information, including the characters and the problems they face," the genie says.

Alisha keys in her summary in the response box on screen and sends the work to be posted to her work log. She logs off and joins her class in a brief discussion of the novel. The following week, Alisha and Ms. Spalding, her teacher, meet to review all of the strategy responses, which have been recorded in a secure online work log. Together they identify examples of effective strategy use. They also identify goals for improvement, such as using more descriptive words in her summaries. But she's making good progress, and Alisha and her teacher decide they are ready to move to a different level of scaffolding—one that provides less structure and will help her become even more independent in reading comprehension.

At the end of the year, Alisha and Ms. Spalding go over all the work she has done for the year and reflect on how much she has grown as a reader. Alisha feels more confident about her abilities as a reader, because the read-aloud feature of the software has allowed her to read the same novel as her classmates and to work on understanding the text rather than decoding. She has also felt more confident about contributing to class discussions, since she could summarize, make predictions, ask questions, and make clarifications with skill. Her growth as a reader is evident in her much-improved performance on the standardized reading assessment.

Alisha's teacher has had a good year, too, especially with the support of a digital learning environment that extended her capacity to address the learning needs of her diverse body of students. With the computer program providing essential supports for decoding text, giving basic explanations of tasks, and keeping records of performance, Ms. Spalding has been able to concentrate on guiding and mentoring students in developing reading comprehension strategies that will help them better understand the varied texts they read in middle school (Dalton, Pisha, Eagleton, Coyne, & Deysher, 2002).

THE CHALLENGE

Reading for meaning is a complex process that must be taught. Once mastered, these skills open opportunities for a lifetime of learning. Yet at all grades and across all subjects, teachers encounter struggling readers. Only 31% of eighth graders are proficient readers, according to the National Assessment of Educational Progress standard for reading proficiency—and just 16% of low-income students and 8% of those with disabilities read at grade level (National Center for Education Statistics, 2009). As students emerge from elementary school and need to read increasingly complex texts to acquire knowledge of specific subject matter, these struggles have the potential to hamper or even reverse their progress in all subject areas. This places a special burden on teachers in the middle and high school grades, who are trying to teach subject matter but are faced with having to provide support for reading comprehension as well.

During the past decade, we have explored ways of making digital reading environments that help struggling readers become strategic readers. Using high-quality novels, chapter books, folktales, informational texts, and picture books, these "scaffolded digital reading environments" (SDRs; see Dalton & Proctor, 2007, 2008) are equipped with learning supports that allow students to interact directly with text in a fashion that is impossible to achieve with static print materials. Our SDRs are designed according to a variety of research-based approaches, including UDL (Rose & Meyer, 2002), reciprocal teaching (Palincsar & Brown, 1984), and robust vocabulary instruction (Beck, McKeown, & Kucan, 2002; Graves, 2006; Nagy, 2009).

We have studied the use of SDRs with heterogeneous learners in elementary and middle school classrooms. Reading achievement results suggest that struggling readers benefit from SDRs, including students with learning disabilities (Dalton, Pisha, Eagleton, Coyne, & Deysher, 2002; Hall & Murray, 2009), those with significant intellectual disabilities (Coyne, Pisha, Dalton, Zeph, & Cook Smith,2010), those who are deaf or hard of hearing (Dalton, Schleper, Kennedy, Lutz, & Strangman, 2005), and those whose first language is not English (Dalton, Proctor, Uccelli, Mo, & Snow, 2011; Proctor, Dalton, & Grisham, 2007; Proctor, Uccelli, Dalton, & Snow, 2009; Proctor et al., 2011).

From a literacy intervention perspective, SDRs are designed such that all students can engage the same texts with embedded supports and scaffolds that vary with the needs of the learner. For example, many intervention studies exclude English language learners (ELLs) because they lack the requisite English proficiency to access the language of text and instruction. In our SDR interventions, however, we can design the texts so that students can access all text, directions, and activities in their native language, as well as English. Thus it is not necessary to exclude ELLs simply because they are learning English (see Proctor et al., 2009). Ultimately, whether students need access to translations, definitions, or comprehension supports, the teacher and students can work together to monitor progress and share the goal of gradually reducing the use of supports as the students become more competent and independent readers. Indeed, excellent readers can hide all features and simply read the digital text as one would a traditional print book.

In this chapter, we share some insights gained from this work, and we offer a framework for designing and using scaffolded digital texts in ways that are sensitive to both traditional reading comprehension processes and the affordances possible in digital environments. In particular, we'll refer to UDL Editions—a set of seven online SDRs freely available for use on a CAST website (*http://udleditions. cast.org*). Developed in partnership with Google and the Carnegie Corporation of New York to celebrate World Book Day 2008, UDL Editions are robust tools that can be used to teach strategies and literary analysis in context, while also providing an individual guided reading experience. The UDL Editions also offer models of how to implement UDL principles in SDRs, which can be helpful whether you are selecting educational digital texts for use in the classroom or designing your own UDL texts with a tool like CAST's UDL Book Builder (*http://bookbuilder.cast.org*). The UDL Edition set includes classic works of literature, including Jack London's *The Call of the Wild*, William Shakespeare's "Sonnet XVIII," Edgar Allan Poe's "The Tell-Tale Heart," and Abraham Lincoln's Gettysburg Address, as well as a retelling of a Native American folktale ("How Coyote Stole Fire") and partner informational text ("All about Coyotes").

THE INTERSECTION OF LITERACY INSTRUCTION AND TECHNOLOGY

Why do some students struggle to read and understand text? The reasons are varied, and have their antecedents in early childhood. Snow, Burns, and Griffin (1998) described "three potential stumbling blocks" that many young children encounter when first learning to read:

The first obstacle, which arises at the outset of reading acquisition, is difficulty understanding and using the alphabetic principle—the idea that written spellings systematically represent spoken words. It is hard to comprehend connected text if word
recognition is inaccurate or laborious. The second obstacle is a failure to transfer the
comprehension skills of spoken language to reading and to acquire new strategies that
may be specifically needed for reading. The third obstacle to reading will magnify
the first two: the absence or loss of an initial motivation to read or failure to develop a
mature appreciation of the rewards of reading. (p.4)

For some students, these early challenges become exacerbated as they progress through school and face increased literacy demands. At the word recognition level, weak decoding and fluency skills are sometimes responsible for affecting
comprehension outcomes. Conceptual and linguistic factors, such as less developed
vocabulary and background knowledge, may deter even a student who possesses
excellent decoding skills from understanding text. Still other readers do not effectively employ strategies for navigating text or monitoring their comprehension.
Struggling readers may face one or more of these hurdles. In fact, research shows
that multiple areas of concern tend to be the rule, not the exception (Fletcher, Lyon,
Fuchs, & Barnes, 2007; Guthrie & Wigfield, 2000); this makes it difficult to improve
reading comprehension, especially for struggling older readers.

In addition, the medium of print is fraught with barriers for struggling readers. Print is fixed and inflexible, a one-size-fits-all medium that is not customizable
to meet individual needs. For example, a fourth grader who struggles to decode
printed words will expend far too much cognitive energy in converting graphic
information into linguistic form (i.e., decoding), when the focus of reading in upper
elementary school and beyond is on acquiring information from a text (LaBerge &
Samuels, 1974). On the other end of the struggling-reader continuum, a student who
is an ELL may be able to decode with native-like accuracy, but may lack the requisite
vocabulary knowledge to make sense of the complex language of secondary texts
(Proctor, Carlo, August, & Snow, 2005). In both cases (and in myriad others), an
inflexible print environment is unable to support these students in the comprehension process.

On the other hand, well-designed digital texts show great promise for supporting struggling readers' developing literacy skills (Dalton & Strangman, 2006). Such
digital texts are malleable and flexible. They can be customized to meet an individual's needs or preferences; they allow for the inclusion of effective scaffolds and
supports that can be activated or withdrawn with relative ease. In short, they can
bend to the needs of diverse learners rather than requiring the learners to bend to
them.

As noted earlier, SDRs are designed according to research-based frameworks,
including reciprocal teaching, robust vocabulary instruction, and UDL. In reciprocal teaching (Palincsar & Brown, 1984), teacher and student discuss a text in an
effort to deepen comprehension of and engagement with the text. This dialogue
is structured around four strategies: predicting, questioning, summarizing, and

clarifying. Visualization and graphic organizers are also often included, as well as strategies for self-monitoring and evaluation. The goal is to release the teacher gradually from the conversation, so that students can independently apply these strategies to develop a deeper understanding of any text. This is important, because good readers are strategic readers. Reciprocal teaching has been implemented successfully with both printed texts (Rosenshine & Meister, 1994) and digital environments (Moran, Ferdig, Pearson, Wardrop, & Blomeyer, 2008).

Research clearly demonstrates that vocabulary knowledge is intricately linked to comprehension; thus comprehension-based approaches to reading generally include some degree of targeted vocabulary instruction. Beck, McKeown, and their colleagues have shown the importance of promoting high-quality vocabulary instruction with both younger and older elementary school children. Over the course of two decades, these researchers have worked with children across the elementary grade spectrum, and have shown strong evidence vocabulary teaching that is "frequent, rich, and extended" (Beck et al., 2002, p. 72) has a positive effect on children's overall word learning and reading comprehension. In these studies, students "identify the relationship between words, respond to words affectively as well as cognitively, and apply words to various contexts" (McKeown, Beck, Omanson, & Pople, 1985, p. 526). These types of activities are ideal for SDRs, as technology makes it possible for students to record their own oral and written responses to words, to see relevant movies and images, and to create their own digital word walls.

In the following section, we describe how the three principles of UDL apply to reading comprehension teaching and learning. In doing so, we use UDL Edition examples to show how these principles are applied in a digital reading environment based on strategy and robust vocabulary instruction.

APPLYING THE UDL PRINCIPLES
TO READING COMPREHENSION INSTRUCTION

UDL draws on insights from brain science and research-based pedagogy (Rose & Meyer, 2002). The three main design principles of UDL as applied to reading are as follows:

I. Provide multiple means of representation—the "what" of reading. What are the words on the page/screen, and what do they mean? This principle corresponds to the recognition networks of the brain.

II. Provide multiple means of action and expression—the "how" of reading. How do I make sense of this text? What strategies do I employ? And how do I express what I know about the text? This principle corresponds to the strategic networks of the brain.

III. Provide multiple means of engagement—the "why" of reading. Why do I care about the text? And why should I continue to stay engaged? This principle corresponds to the affective networks of the brain.

Though presented here as three distinct items, these principles are, like their corresponding brain networks, part of a highly integrated system. A deficit in any one area may lead to reading struggles. However, for the purposes of clarity, it helps to look at each individual principle, identify potential barriers to reading success, and consider how practical applications of the UDL Guidelines will address those concerns. We use the UDL Editions as examples, and we refer throughout to the UDL Guidelines (see CAST, 2011).

Principle I: Provide Multiple Means of Representation

Reading comprehension depends on the recognition of words and their meaning. At its most basic, this requires decoding the words on the page. But comprehension also requires much more: a connection to prior (or background) knowledge; an adequate vocabulary; an appreciation for the context in which words appear; and some knowledge of the varied text structures that accompany instruction at the upper elementary and middle grades (Fang & Schleppegrell, 2008). Thus recognition in a reading context requires that words be correctly decoded, then mapped to an existing understanding of word meanings, syntax, grammar, and background knowledge, all within a given academic domain. The UDL Guidelines address these needs in the following ways:

• *UDL Guideline 1 suggests providing multiple options for perception.* For many readers who struggle to decode text or have trouble with fluency, text-to-speech (TTS) software provides essential access support, so that these readers can better focus on understanding content. TTS software allows students to click on a word, phrase, or passage and have it read aloud. Each UDL Edition enables TTS capability through a special toolbar provided by TextHelp. Text is read aloud in a synthetic voice and is accompanied by synchronized highlighting. Students can select their own voice and narration rate, and are asked to read along in the text as they are listening to the TTS read-aloud, so that they are both seeing and hearing the words simultaneously. CAST's UDL Editions also enable other supports for perception, including the ability to change text size, fonts, and colors—something a printed text would not allow.

In their work with individuals who are deaf or hard of hearing, Dalton et al. (2005) embedded American Sign Language (ASL) video and Signing Avatar clips (VCom3D) in SDRs for middle school students. Students could click on a word or passage and view it signed in ASL. In this case, the "reading" of the word was necessarily connected to its meaning, since ASL is a fully developed language system where the sign and meaning are interrelated (finger spelling is an exception). Although the UDL Editions do not include this feature, we include it here to illustrate further how providing options for recognition (i.e., ASL) can support reading comprehension for individuals with diverse learning needs.

• *UDL Guideline 2 calls for options for language and symbols,* especially vocabulary, languages other than English, and other representational supports. If students do not have access to word meaning (vocabulary), they cannot access text meaning. For example, each challenging word in a UDL Edition is hyperlinked to a pop-up window with the word, a definition, the word used in a sentence to provide context, and often an image. Literary devices, such as the use of metaphor or irony, are also hyperlinked to explanations of their use in the particular text context. In addition, every word in a UDL Edition can be translated into Spanish via a TextHelp toolbar that is always one click away. In related research, we (Dalton et al., 2011; Proctor et al., 2007, 2009, 2011) designed an SDR to support schools and classes with large percentages of Spanish–English bilingual learners, and thus provided access to all text, directions, and activities in Spanish as well as English.

• *UDL Guideline 3 calls for options for comprehension.* In addition to having access to the words and their meanings, readers need to put those meaningful words in context and recognize what is important in a text. Even readers who do not struggle with decoding and word meanings may wrestle to comprehend a text because of other factors, such as context and culture.

For example, young 21st-century readers may struggle to understand the issues or rhetorical devices in a text such as Jack London's *The Call of the Wild*, written in 1903. Differences in language, history, culture, and era may make this text difficult to read even when discrete words and word meanings are understood. Historical allusions, customs, and colloquialisms of the Alaskan Gold Rush can all make the speech a challenging text for modern readers. The UDL Edition of *The Call of the Wild* (London, 1903/2011) addresses this by linking to high-quality informational websites about the Gold Rush, the Yukon, sled dogs, and wolves. These links are designed both to build background knowledge to help clarify the text, and to provide opportunities for extension and enrichment.

Principle II: Provide Multiple Means of Action and Expression

Successful reading requires much more than recognizing the elements of language. It requires implementing effective strategies and tactics for constructing meaning from texts. To do so, readers draw on the brain networks that control the planning, organizing, and execution of tasks. In an academic context, successful reading also frequently involves articulating or demonstrating one's understanding of a text through note taking, writing, oral discussion, or other tasks.

• *UDL Guideline 4 calls for providing options for physical action.* For example, readers of the UDL Editions have easy access to a TextHelp toolbar, which allows them to highlight and paste text or images into a word processor. This can help them as they compose a reflection on the text.

The TextHelp feature also supports *UDL Guideline 5, which urges options for expressive skills and fluency*—not just in the physical means of expression, but also in the method of expression. TextHelp can support readers in organizing and composing their response to the text. The sentence starters, probing questions, and examples included in the program can also help scaffold the process of response to reading.

• *UDL Guideline 6 suggests support for a reader's executive functions*—that is, the skills of setting goals, making plans and strategies to achieve those goals, and monitoring progress toward those goals. Skilled, independent readers do this routinely without having to give it a lot of thought. In approaching Edgar Allan Poe's "The Tell-Tale Heart," readers may apply their knowledge of horror films to the text, taking note of clues signaling the conflict and possibilities of revenge. Or they may develop a sketch of the two main characters as preparation for a multimedia poster they are creating about the story.

Struggling readers need support in developing executive functions, and UDL Editions provide this in a number of ways (see Figure 3.1). Throughout the text, readers are asked to "Stop and Think." They may then be asked to employ a reading strategy—that is, to make predictions, raise questions, summarize the text, or

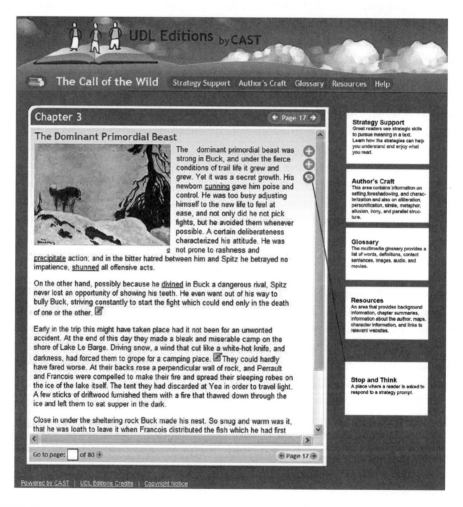

FIGURE 3.1. UDL Editions support readers in developing reading comprehension strategies, background knowledge, and executive functions. From London (1903/2011). Copyright 2011 by CAST, Inc. All rights reserved. Used with permission.

visualize the narrative. Other prompts help develop awareness of the author's craft, providing exercises based in the text that enhance the reader's understanding of narrative elements (such as setting, characterization, and foreshadowing) or literary devices (allusion, personification, simile/metaphor, etc.). To scaffold the development of such skills, readers can choose one of three levels of support. Those who select the most support may be asked to choose one of three prewritten and specific predictions ("I predict that Buck will start having nightmares . . . "), while those who select less support may be prompted in an open-ended way ("Make a prediction! Use the Text Help toolbar above to highlight and collect clues—important words and phrases—to help you make a prediction"). The goal is to release scaffolds and supports gradually, so that readers become more independent—the way a novice bicyclist eventually takes off the training wheels. For each prompt, an animated "coach" is ready to provide a model response or clarify the task at hand.

Principle III: Provide Multiple Means of Engagement

Successful readers are *active and engaged* in the reading process. They are persistent. They know how to assess their progress and adjust their goals and strategies accordingly. They maintain a sense of purpose about reading, and they remain determined to finish a text and draw some value from it. An SDR that is based on UDL principles makes reading more engaging, fun, and challenging in appropriate ways.

• *UDL Guideline 7 suggests the need to actively recruit readers' interest.* Readers need to know that their reading has a real purpose—that it's not just "something you have to do." One way to recruit interest is to give students choice and independence in what they read or the supports they can use. CAST's UDL Editions accomplish this by allowing readers to choose the level of support they receive. Students also have control over whether to use audio, what colors to use for highlighting, and so forth. These options give the text a more customized "feel" than a standard printed book would allow, thus increasing engagement for some readers.

Another way to recruit interest is to increase the relevance, value, and authenticity of the reading. One way our UDL Editions do this is to use classic literature as a means of connecting readers to contemporary sources. The Web makes this possible. For example, readers of *The Call of the Wild* can track Buck's travels by using Google Maps—or can even get directions from their homes to the locations in the novel that Buck visits (Figure 3.2). Readers of Lincoln's Gettysburg Address can view photographs of the battle's devastation and compare them to current war photography. Even a small personal connection can make the reader more engaged in the text.

• *UDL Guideline 8 calls for providing options for sustaining effort and persistence.* Reading requires sustained attention. However, individuals differ in their ability to stay focused on a text. Sometimes frustration gets in the way, if a text is too

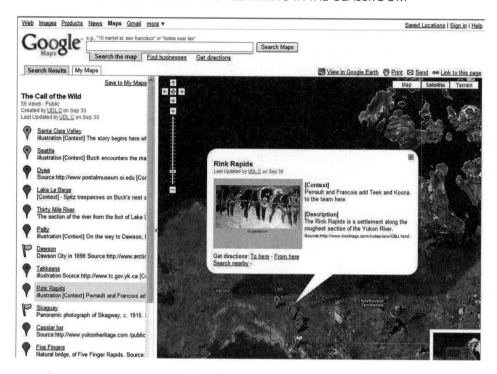

FIGURE 3.2. UDL Editions connect readers of classic literature to contemporary sources, thus increasing reader engagement. For example, readers of *The Call of the Wild* can track Buck's travels by using Google Maps—or can even get directions from their homes to the locations in the novel that Buck visits. From London (1903/2011). Copyright 2011 by CAST, Inc. All rights reserved. Used with permission.

challenging. At other times, boredom is the problem: The text is not challenging enough. An SDR based on UDL principles provides options that can help stave off boredom, frustration, or other impediments to persistence, including appropriate supports and challenges. With our UDL Editions, the "just-in-time" feature supports all work to sustain effort and persistence, and the option of selecting types and levels of supports, depending on reading comprehension skill, also serves to help readers avoid boredom and frustration. Easily accessible word definitions, translations, background information, note-taking tools, strategy supports, models, and "coaches" all make the text more user-friendly. So too does the TTS feature. These features enable the reader to stay with the text longer without having to reach for a dictionary or reference book.

- *UDL Guideline 9 calls for providing options for self-regulation.* Ultimately, skilled readers know how to sustain interest and attention themselves, and independence is the goal of any UDL-based reading environment. What happens if readers do not know a word? What is interesting to them, and how can they leverage that to accomplish the task? And they need to be reflective about their reading. This means they have to be able to evaluate their own work, and think about what they have done well and not so well. The leveled supports in our UDL Editions support this kind of self-regulation, allowing readers to raise and lower the level of challenge in applying strategies. Other SDRs, such as the MassONE Writer described in Chapter 4, offer the option of recording reader responses in online work logs. This enables teachers and students together to better monitor progress and reflect on the reading process.

Finally, the fact that UDL Editions are online makes it possible to extend the supported reading experience after school hours and outside the school building. Wherever readers can get online, they can access the text and have all of the "teaching" supports that typically would be provided by an expert instructor—at a time and place of their choosing.

LITERACY FOR THE DIGITAL AGE

As new technologies evolve, so too does our definition of literacy. "Literacy" means something quite different today than it did even a decade ago. However, few would dispute that the old slogan "Reading is fundamental" is still relevant—and true. A report on digital media from Sesame Workshop (Shore, 2008) declared:

> In the global, interconnected world children inhabit, they must come to terms with many ideas and master many new competencies. And yet, it remains vitally important to become literate in the traditional sense of being "lettered"—able to decipher and make meaning from written texts. (p. 27)

Technology can play an important role in helping "digital natives" (Prensky, 2001) become fluent readers of texts. An SDR that is designed according to UDL principles really offers an easier way (and, for certain learners, the only feasible means) of supporting all kinds of readers in developing their skills. The flexibility and malleability of digital text is critical to providing many learners with basic access to such texts—learners who would otherwise be shut out by the technology of print (Meyer & Rose, 2005). But digital environments offer much more than mere access when they are designed according to UDL principles. As this chapter has shown, these texts can be rendered in exciting, engaging ways that include lots of structure and supports for readers. This has the potential to relieve teachers of providing some of that basic support and structure, and to free them up to do what they do best: providing targeted interventions for those who are especially struggling to stay at grade level. They can also use UDL Editions and a projector to introduce and teach specific strategies and literary analysis to the whole class or small groups, followed by having individuals or partners work on the computer reading the texts as guided practice before tackling other texts on their own. Some may be encouraged to create their own digital texts with the help of CAST's free authoring tool, UDL Book Builder. Technology will never replace teachers, but it can help them focus and target their efforts more effectively. Most importantly, it can level the playing field for struggling readers and offer new opportunities for becoming successful readers and learners.

REFERENCES

Beck, I. L., McKeown, M. G., & Kucan, L. (2002). *Bringing words to life.* New York: Guilford Press.

CAST. (2011). *Universal Design for Learning Guidelines version 2.0.* Wakefield, MA: Author. Retrieved February 22, 2012, from *http://www.udlcenter.org/aboutudl/udlguidelines.*

Coyne, P., Pisha, B., Dalton, B., Zeph, L., & Cook Smith, N. (2010). Literacy by design: A Universal Design for Learning approach for students with significant intellectual disabilities. *Remedial and Special Education.* Retrieved September 30, 2010, from *http://rse. sagepub.com/content/early/2010/08/30/0741932510381651.*

Dalton, B., Pisha, B., Eagleton, M., Coyne, P., & Deysher, S. (2002). *Engaging the text: Reciprocal teaching and questioning strategies in a scaffolded learning environment* (Final report to the U.S. Department of Education). Peabody, MA: CAST.

Dalton, B., & Proctor, C. P. (2007). Reading as thinking: Integrating strategy instruction in a universally designed digital literacy environment. In D. S. McNamara (Ed.), *Reading comprehension strategies: Theories, interventions, and technologies* (pp. 421–440). Mahwah, NJ: Erlbaum.

Dalton, B., & Proctor, C. P. (2008). The changing landscape of text and comprehension in the age of new literacies. In J. Coiro, M. Knobel, C. Lankshear, & D. Leu (Eds.), *Handbook of research on new literacies* (pp. 297–324). Mahwah, NJ: Erlbaum.

Dalton, B., Proctor, C. P., Uccelli, P., Mo, E. & Snow, C. E. (2011). Designing for diversity: The role of reading strategies and interactive vocabulary in a digital reading environment for 5th grade monolingual English and bilingual students. *Journal of Literacy Research, 43*(1), 68–100.

Dalton, B., Schleper, D., Kennedy, M., Lutz, L., & Strangman, N. (2005). *A universally designed digital strategic reading environment for adolescents who are deaf and hard of hearing* (Final report to Gallaudet University). Wakefield, MA: CAST.

Dalton, B., & Strangman, N. (2006). Improving struggling readers' comprehension through scaffolded hypertexts and other computer-based literacy programs. In D. Reinking, M.C. McKenna, L. D. Labbo, & R.D. Keiffer (Eds.), *Handbook of literacy and technology* (2nd ed., pp. 75–92). Mahwah, NJ: Erlbaum.

Fang, Z., & Schleppegrell, M. J. (2008). *Reading in secondary content areas: A language-based pedagogy.* Ann Arbor: University of Michigan Press.

Fletcher, J. M., Lyon, G. R., Fuchs, L. S., & Barnes, M. A. (2007). *Learning disabilities: From identification to intervention.* New York: Guilford Press.

Graves, M. F. (2006). *The vocabulary book: Learning and instruction.* New York: Teachers College Press.

Guthrie, J. T., & Wigfield, A. (2000). Engagement and motivation in reading. In M. L. Kamil, P. B. Mosenthal, P. D. Pearson, & R. Barr (Eds.), *Handbook of reading research* (Vol. 3, pp. 403–422). New York: Routledge.

Hall, T. E., & Murray, E. (2009). *Monitoring students' progress towards standards in reading: A universally designed CBM system* (Final project report to the U.S. Department of Education). Wakefield, MA: CAST.

LaBerge, D., & Samuels, J. (1974). Towards a theory of automatic information processing in reading. *Cognitive Psychology, 6,* 293–323.

London, J. (2011). *The call of the wild* (UDL Edition). Wakefield, MA: CAST. (Original work published 1903) Retrieved from *http://udleditions.cast.org/INTRO,call_of_the_wild.html.*

McKeown, M. G., Beck, I. L., Omanson, R. C., & Pople, M. T. (1985). Some effects of the nature and frequency of vocabulary instruction on the knowledge and use of words. *Reading Research Quarterly, 20,* 522–535.

Meyer, A., & Rose, D. H. (2005). The future is in the margins: The role of technology and disability in educational reform. In D. H. Rose, A. Meyer, & C. Hitchcock (Eds.), *The universally designed classroom: Accessible curriculum and digital technologies* (pp. 13–35). Cambridge, MA: Harvard Education Press.

Moran, J., Ferdig, R. E., Pearson, P. D., Wardrop, J., & Blomeyer, Jr., R. L. (2008). Technology and reading performance in the middle-school grades: A meta-analysis with recommendations for policy and practice. *Journal of Literacy Research, 40*(1), 6–58.

Nagy, W. (2009). Understanding words and word learning: Putting research on vocabulary into classroom practice. In S. Rosenfield & V. Berninger (Eds.), *Implementing evidence-based academic interventions in school settings* (pp. 479–500). New York: Oxford University Press.

National Center for Education Statistics. (2009). *The nation's report card: Reading 2009.* Washington, DC: Author.

Palincsar, A.S., & Brown, A.L. (1984). Reciprocal teaching of comprehension-fostering and comprehension-monitoring activities. *Cognition and Instruction, 1,* 117–175.

Paulsen, G. (1999). *Hatchet.* New York: Aladdin.

Prensky, M. (2001). Digital natives, digital immigrants. *On the Horizon, 9*(5), 1–6. Retrieved September 30, 2010, from *http://www.marcprensky.com/writing/Prensky%20-%20Digital%20Natives,%20Digital%20Immigrants%20-%20Part1.pdf.*

Proctor, C. P., Carlo, M. S., August, D., & Snow, C. E. (2005). Native Spanish-speaking children reading in English: Towards a model of comprehension. *Journal of Educational Psychology, 97*(2), 246–256.

Proctor, C. P., Dalton, B., & Grisham, D. L. (2007). Scaffolding English language learners and struggling readers in a universal literacy environment with embedded strategy instruction and vocabulary support. *Journal of Literacy Research, 39*(1), 71–93.

Proctor, C. P., Dalton, B., Uccelli, P., Biancarosa, G., Mo, E., Snow, C. E. et al. (2011). Improving comprehension online: Effects of deep vocabulary instruction with bilingual and monolingual fifth graders. *Reading and Writing: An Interdisciplinary Journal, 24*(5), 517–544.

Proctor, C. P., Uccelli, P., Dalton, B., & Snow, C. E. (2009). Understanding depth of vocabulary and improving comprehension online with bilingual and monolingual children. *Reading and Writing Quarterly, 25*(4), 311–333.

Rose, D. H., & Meyer, A. (2002). *Teaching every student in the digital age: Universal Design for Learning.* Alexandria, VA: Association for Supervision and Curriculum Development.

Rosenshine, B., & Meister, C. (1994). Reciprocal teaching: A review of the research. *Review of Educational Research, 64*(4), 479–530.

Shore, R. (2008). *The power of Pow! Wham!: Children, digital media, and our nation's future. Three challenges for the coming decade.* New York: Joan Ganz Cooney Center at Sesame Workshop.

Snow, C. E., Burns, M. S., & Griffin, P. (1998). *Preventing reading difficulties in young children.* Washington, DC: National Academy Press.

CHAPTER 4

Transforming Writing Instruction with Universal Design for Learning

GE VUE and TRACEY E. HALL

Writing is an essential literacy skill and a key to academic achievement across the curriculum. From middle school on, most subjects require students to demonstrate their understanding and progress through writing. Students must develop the ability to synthesize what they read, formulate new ideas, and express their conceptions and thoughts through writing. In many states and districts, they must also demonstrate writing proficiency in order to graduate and move on to college (College Board, 2008). Yet evidence shows that the gap between students' writing skills and competency standards is significant. Results from the 2007 National Assessment of Educational Progress revealed that 69% of eighth-grade students scored below "proficient" (National Center for Education Statistics, 2008).

The need to write well doesn't end with graduation. Writing is highly valued in our culture; it is a leading criterion for how we are judged in the workplace. Today's digital world employs a wide range of tools for communication, collaboration, creative expression, and lifelong learning. Nearly all require effective writing skills; email, discussion forums, blogs, and collaborative writing applications such as Google Docs and wikis are just a few of the venues (Johnson, Levine, Smith, & Stone, 2010). All of these tools privilege individuals who can transform their ideas into written words. Students who develop effective writing skills in their school years will enter adulthood with a significant advantage over those who do not express themselves well in written words.

THE CHALLENGES OF LEARNING TO WRITE
AND TEACHING WRITING

Writing is hard work and is difficult to master. Why? Because writing is counter-intuitive to how our brains work. Our brains are multimodal. We visualize ideas. Thoughts float in and out of our heads—and rarely in a linear way. Writing attempts to shape that free-forming, dynamic process of thought into a single, linear output of sentences and paragraphs that are logical, concise, and clear. No wonder novice writers have sweaty palms, shaky hands, and chattering teeth when facing a writing assignment. They have all these creative ideas in their imaginative minds, but because their minds are so much quicker and richer than their pens, the outcome when they put ink to paper is a blank sheet.

Research shows a lack of effective writing instruction across the curriculum. Content-area teachers focus primarily on teaching their particular areas; they generally do not explicitly teach students how to write. Yet writing skills transcend traditional subject categories, and students are expected to come to class with writing as a skill set that can be used to learn new content and to demonstrate their knowledge of complex concepts (Gersten & Baker, 2001; Olson, 2011; Stein, Dixon, & Barnard, 2001). Tests are common methods of assessing students' progress, but many content-area teachers also grade students' performance on the basis of written reports. Writing tasks, with supported instruction, across the curriculum give students more opportunity to practice writing. Imagine how much more students' writing skills could improve if they also received explicit instruction and feedback on writing for different disciplines.

Robert McKee (1997), a famous screenwriting instructor, says that writing "is about principles, not rules; universal form, not formula; originality, not duplication" (p. 3). McKee uses these terms to distinguish the mechanics of writing from the art of writing, and he thus captures the challenge of teaching writing. There are no hard-and-fast rules, no one-size-fits-all approach. Writing is highly stylistic. In fact, the mark of an expert writer is one who not only can use written words to communicate clearly, but can do so in his or her own unique voice.

Writing skills are also context-specific (Graham & Perin, 2007). There are enough differences among various forms of composition that competency in one form won't automatically make one an equal expert in another. To master narrative, one needs to study expert models of narratives and to practice writing narratives (Graham & Harris, 2000; Langer, 2009). To become a poet, one needs to study the work of expert poets and to practice writing poetry. There are no shortcuts or quick fixes.

To ease students' fear and anxiety, some teachers employ a scaffolded strategy to teach writing. Much as they might provide training wheels for a child learning to ride a bicycle, teachers provide students with a structure—a progressive sequence of steps called *process writing*. This approach breaks the writing process into four discrete steps: (1) clarify, (2) precompose, (3) compose, and (4) publish. Students are taught each step and ways to apply the steps when writing. Despite this discrete sequence of steps, however, process writing is not a linear progression, but an iterative cycle of planning, writing, and rewriting. Process writing is also not a recipe; there is no one right place or one right way to begin or end the process. At best, the process serves as a scaffold that is gradually removed as students master their skills, like training wheels. For novice writers, process writing can be very helpful or downright perplexing. Not only are the individual differences of writers a challenge to address, but teachers' approaches, styles and instructional practices vary greatly also.

UNIVERSAL DESIGN FOR LEARNING AS A BASIS FOR TEACHING WRITING

As the preceding discussion indicates, teaching writing and learning to write are difficult because the scaffolds and supports that learners need to become expert writers vary by tasks, forms of writing, and individuals. Fortunately, these challenges to writing instruction happen to be strengths of Universal Design for Learning (UDL). The UDL principles are based on the fact that learners differ in how they comprehend information (recognition networks), how they express what they know (strategic networks), and how they can be motivated to learn (affective networks) (see Hall, Meyer, & Rose, Chapter 1, and Lapinski, Gravel, & Rose, Chapter 2, this volume). Effective instruction in any area starts with setting clear learning goals and then providing enough variety and options to help all learners reach them. The three UDL principles and the corresponding UDL Guidelines (CAST, 2011; see Chapter 2) can thus be effectively applied to improve writing instruction.

In the information age, the tools for writing and for teaching writing have changed dramatically, yielding a wide range of tools and media to enable students to write, receive support, hone their skills, and pursue their writing goals (Johnson et al., 2010). In other words, educators can now provide students with multiple methods for comprehending the elements and steps of writing (representation), for transforming ideas into words (expression and action), and for inspiring and sustaining the desire to write (affective engagement) throughout the writing process.

The UDL Guidelines will help educators to set high expectations, yet include enough flexibility to permit writers to take different paths toward producing high-quality writing, developing their own voices, and applying writing as a lifelong set of skills. The Guidelines are very comprehensive, so teachers may find that only applying some, not all, will provide enough flexibility to support all learners. Rather than refer to each and every UDL Guideline in this chapter, we instead highlight three learning design strategies derived from the Guidelines that work together to improve the teaching and learning of writing:

1. Set clear writing goals. The goals should not specify the means to reach them.
2. Provide appropriate challenges and flexible means to achieve the goals.
3. Engage learners and sustain their motivation to write by providing choices

in writing topics, tools for creative expression, and forms of writing, as long as these choices do not undermine or conflict with the learning goals.

To show what these strategies looking like in practice, we share classroom examples drawn from CAST's work with teachers in applying UDL. In the first example, CAST collaborated with the Massachusetts Department of Education to build a highly supportive web-based learning environment called MassONE Writer that applies the UDL principles to writing instruction and classroom practices. The second example showcases how a middle school English language arts (ELA) teacher recruits and sustains the engagement of her students by giving them a compelling reason to learn persuasive writing, and provides various scaffolds and strategies to enable them to do this. The third example describes how two high school teachers from different departments have collaborated to design an interdisciplinary curriculum that improves writing and learning across content areas. Each example is followed by an analysis of how the three UDL strategies have been applied across different learning settings.

TRANSFORMING WRITING INSTRUCTION WITH UDL AND WEB-BASED TECHNOLOGY: MassONE WRITER

"If the process is sound, the outcome will take care of itself," writes notable author and writing teacher William Zinsser (1988, p. 256). Writing is hard work, and worrying about the final product is counterproductive. Instead, Zinsser instructs young writers to study effective models and practice imitating them. However, research shows that current instructional practices employing process writing provide inconsistent models as supports and few opportunities to practice (Graham, MacArthur, & Fitzgerald, 2007). Feedback from both teachers and peers is essential to developing writing skills and an understanding of good writing. Yet the constraints of a school setting (time, large class size, and curricular restrictions) leave little time for teachers and students to interact and discuss student writing.

To address these concerns, CAST partnered with the Massachusetts Department of Education to develop a prototype online learning environment that would support students in learning and practicing the writing process. This tool, MassONE Writer, designed for a proof-of-concept study, combines two effective models of writing instruction widely used in middle school—process writing and writer's workshop. As noted earlier, process writing breaks the writing process into concrete steps: (1) clarify, (2) precompose, (3) compose, and (4) publish. Students learn to apply each step strategically as they compose (Applebee & Langer, 2006). Writer's workshop embeds the process of writing into a learning community in which students frequently stop to analyze and provide feedback on each other's work (e.g., Gabriel, 2002). The writer's workshop model embraces writing as a social activity in which the learning community makes key contributions to the writer's development. CAST applied the UDL principles of design and the flexibility of web-based technology to provide multiple ways for learners to comprehend the elements of process writing (recognition/representation); multiple opportunities to practice writing (expression and action) in a highly supportive learning environment; and choices of writing topics, tools, and settings to motivate and sustain their engagement throughout the writing process. The following brief description of MassONE Writer highlights these UDL features.

Providing Multiple Representations of the Writing Process

To help students learn the elements of writing, MassONE Writer provides a visual display of the process writing structure, which also serves as the main navigation menu. At each stage, both a short description and a checklist of writing elements are provided (see Figure 4.1). Text-to-speech (TTS) software is available to read aloud information on the page or text that students wrote. This provides students with the option to read or listen to the information on the page. The multiple representation of the writing process supports students to understand the goals and expectations of the writing assignment.

Providing Multiple Means of Strategic Learning and Expression

To guide the development of competence and expertise in emerging writers, MassONE Writer provides opportunity for guided practice with scaffolds and feedback. The writing process is organized into manageable stages, to help students focus attention on writing one section at a time. Prompts and sentence starters are

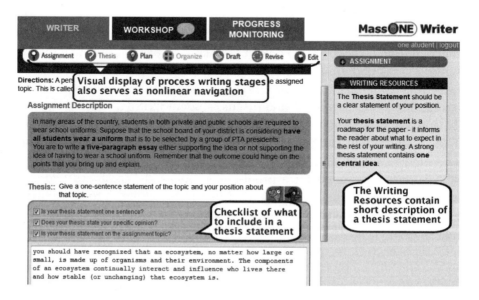

FIGURE 4.1. A screenshot of MassONE Writer. The callouts highlight the multiple representations of information on process writing—a visual display of the stages, a checklist, and a short description. Copyright 2011 by CAST, Inc. All rights reserved. Used with permission.

available to help students put their ideas into words. At each stage, models pertaining to that stage (e.g., a clearly stated thesis or logically structured arguments) are also provided. Complete writing samples by past students are available for students to learn from and emulate. A checklist reminds students to review their drafts and includes essential writing elements. At any time, students can post sections of their writing to "Workshop"—a collaborative workspace where both the teacher and their peers can read what they wrote and provide feedback. Discussing real examples of peer writing online is a great opportunity to practice writing by communicating and interacting with classmates. Workshop has strategies and tips for critiquing drafts and providing meaningful feedback.

Providing Multiple Means of Engagement

MassONE Writer addresses learners' motivation and engagement in several ways. As just described, it provides scaffolds—sentence starters, checklists, and models—to reduce the challenges and fear of writing. The scaffolds are genre-specific, allowing students to choose any topic and still find them contextually relevant. The preference and permission settings offer students choices of tools, audience, and format for writing and feedback. They can write online or can use a desktop word processor like Microsoft Word and then upload the draft to MassONE Writer for feedback or publication. They can share their compositions as unlisted, so that only individuals with whom they've shared the link will be able to access them, or they can make the compositions public for anyone on the Web to read them. They can complete writing assignments independently and still have instant access to writing scaffolds as needed, or can write collaboratively and receive additional support from peers. And Workshop provides students with the option to provide and receive feedback through face-to-face conferencing in the classroom or online. When used strategically, the wide range of scaffolds and preferences in MassONE Writer can help to sustain learners' motivation and engagement throughout the writing process.

Teaching with MassONE Writer

This description of MassONE Writer illustrates how the UDL Guidelines can be applied to designing curricular materials and instruction (see Figure 4.2). Nevertheless, well-designed materials and flexible web-based technology alone do not make a classroom an example of "UDL." Teachers must also apply the principles of UDL throughout the implementation and evaluation of their teaching. For example, while some students work independently in MassONE Writer, a teacher can spend extra time working with other students who may feel frustrated, or can ask students who can support each other to work together. Peer feedback in Workshop is effective for improving both the quality of a composition and the skills of its writer, but providing meaningful feedback is a challenge for many students. Since all student work is stored on a Web server, the teacher can easily pull out samples of students' writing from previous classes, project them on a classroom screen, and

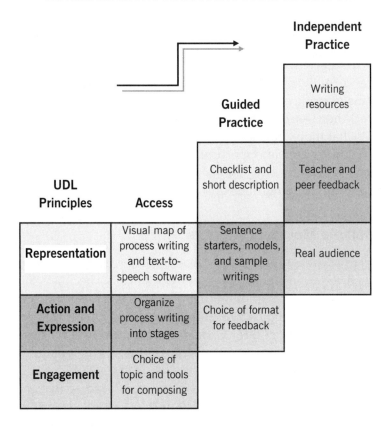

FIGURE 4.2. A visual summary of the UDL features in MassONE Writer. The UDL features are organized by principles and displayed visually as steps, to emphasize the progression of scaffolds for practice and performance that help novice learners grow into expert writers.

model different feedback strategies. The teacher can also model critiquing and providing feedback by working through examples together with the class. Then students can practice applying the strategies by analyzing and providing feedback on each other's compositions—putting checkmarks next to sentences or paragraphs that are well written, highlighting or summarizing the main idea in a paragraph, asking clarifying and probing questions, and suggesting concrete changes. As students' skills develop, they can evaluate their own work and learning processes, thus becoming more self-reflective about the quality of their work and effort throughout the writing process.

Teachers reported that students who had struggled to complete a single piece of writing were able to complete their first essays when they used MassONE Writer. Other students, who were already familiar with writing and revising their work by using supports commonly available in word processors (such as TTS software, spell checker, thesaurus, and dictionary), were ecstatic to discover a richer array of learning supports in MassONE Writer. Students who were infrequent or reluctant participants in classroom dialogues were posting valuable feedback to their

TRANSFORMING WRITING INSTRUCTION WITH UDL AND WEB-BASED TECHNOLOGY

Because MassONE Writer is a prototype, it is not yet available for public use. However, there are web-based office suites and website authoring applications that can support most of the UDL features we've described. These applications allow users to use a Web browser to create, edit, and share documents or webpages stored on a server. Some have design templates with navigation menus, page layouts, and color schemes to choose from. Some also have a simple discussion forum that can be set up to support a writer's workshop. Most have a free version for users to get started, and then an option to upgrade to a fee-based version as their needs grow.

- Twiki: *http://twiki.org*
- Wikispaces: *http://www.wikispaces.com*
- PBworks: *http://pbworks.com*
- Ning: *http://www.ning.com*
- Google Site: *http://www.google.com/sites/overview.html*
- Google Docs: *http://www.google.com/google-d-s/documents*
- Office Web Apps: *http://office.microsoft.com/en-us/web-apps*

peers. The extensive writing supports in MassONE Writer guided the development of competence and expertise in emerging writers; enabled students to engage in writing as a collaborative, social activity; and provided a distribution platform for student writings to reach a wider audience.

LEARNING PERSUASIVE WRITING: JFK MIDDLE SCHOOL

Classes are changing at JFK Middle School. Lockers bang shut, voices echo in the long hallways, and feet pound as students head to their next class. At the ELA classroom door, Ms. Stevens greets her students with a stern look and hands them an assignment sheet. As the students file into the classroom and read the assignment, their light-hearted mood fades into puzzled and concerned frowns.

"It's spring, and it's time for a change in my classroom," Ms. Stevens says firmly. "The paper you received at the door is a listing of our new rules. I'm tired of late assignments. I don't want to hear people talking out of turn, or being rude to one another or to me any longer. So, after thinking a lot about your behavior and our goals, I decided we need a change. These new rules will take effect immediately and run until the end of the year. Take a few minutes to read the list of rules and look up at me when you are finished." Shock registers on the students' faces as they read silently.

After a few minutes, Ms. Stevens acknowledges the severity of the new rules. In fact, she is going to give them an opportunity to speak out. Each student may identify one rule that he or she thinks is unfair and should be changed. There is a catch, though: They need to describe *in writing* what is wrong with the rule, how the rule should be changed, and why. Ms. Stevens writes these steps on the whiteboard and instructs the class to take out pencils and paper. "If you convince me that your change is good, then I may consider revising the rule," she assures them.

After a few minutes of feverish writing, the students began putting their pencils down and looking toward the front of the class. Ms. Stevens calls on one to read his composition. "I wrote about the new Rule 2—'No one may speak in class without permission.' I wrote: 'I urge you to change this rule, Ms. Stevens. Not having permission to talk will make class discussions too difficult.'" Upon completion of the reading, Ms. Stevens explains that what he wrote *was* a clear statement. However, a good argument must have both a statement *and* supporting evidence. She then invites the class to provide reasons to support the rule change and prompts them to provide evidence. Here are some of their comments:

- "Class discussion is about conversation about books or poems we read. Stopping conversation to get permission to talk will make it impossible to really talk about what we're thinking. We can't always remember."
- "Yeah, we can share ideas and pay attention to each other. Waiting for permission will slow us down."
- Sometimes we get noisy—once in a while—but we are working and enjoying talking to each other. Don't stop that!"

Ms. Stevens agrees that her students have provided good reasons to support the argument. She invites her students to look at their statements about various other rules and add or change them to include the reasons that support *why* they would change a particular rule.

As students continue modifying their writing and sharing it, Ms. Stevens provides immediate feedback by modeling how to structure a good argument. She also encourages them to practice by revising what they wrote: She allows them to scratch out, erase, or start a fresh sheet of paper as they make changes to the statements and develop arguments.

Feeling confident that her students now know what an argument is and how to construct one, she notifies them that they have indeed persuaded her to reconsider the rules. Their persuasive arguments with clear rationales and emotional engagement have convinced her to adopt some of the recommended modifications. The students appear pleased and relieved.

Then, with a giant smile on her face, Ms. Stevens announces that they will not be changing any rules. Instead, the class will finally start using an online forum to discuss the book they have been reading. "The purpose of this exercise was to prepare you to write coherent posts," she says. "The forum is not a place to chat and post messages to your friends. When responding to a discussion question or a post, I expect you to use the strategies you have practiced. A good argument must be clearly stated and include evidence from the reading."

To master the art of an argument, the students need more opportunities to practice with feedback and with different topics and contexts. Thus Ms. Stevens initiates this online forum where students can discuss their work and provide peer feedback. In the forum, long posts with multiple arguments are discouraged, because they are difficult to reply to and often stifle instead of deepen discussion. This makes the forum an ideal tool for learning to argue, because it encourages students to include one thoughtful argument per post. Ms. Stevens can follow the students' conversations on the forum; she can also read students' arguments and evaluate them for logic and coherence in relation to the topic. Such a forum is great for teachers because all student work is aggregated in one place on the Web, making it quick and easy to review and provide feedback from any location that has Internet access, and enabling students to contribute even when they're not in school. The forum creates a record and thus a means to evaluate responses and reactions in writing. Teachers are also able to shape the writing of comments and feedback during instruction, and to view the impact of that instruction in the next conversation. This archive of student dialogue in writing literally houses the progression of students' writing skills over time. The more experience students have in writing their arguments, the more clearly they articulate the meaning they are trying to convey.

The results are remarkable in Ms. Stevens's classroom. Students who were not previously writing papers required for class soon become active participants in the forum. Peers encourage one another to write by posting comments to their topics. Periodically, the class holds face-to-face discussions to review what makes an appropriate forum topic and how to construct good open-ended questions that drive online discussions. Ms. Stevens reads all student posts, and occasionally nudges some students to respond to other classmates and not just to their friends. She wants her students to feel that the discussion forum is their space, and to take responsibility for themselves and each other when they are online. Overall, the forum experience is very satisfying for Ms. Stevens as a teaching and evaluation or monitoring tool, as well as a motivating activity for students. Ms. Stevens remarks that her students even ask to go on the forum during occasional free time in class.

Using State Standards and UDL Strategies for Teaching Persuasive Writing

The UDL strategies described earlier in this chapter recommend setting clear goals but keeping the means to achieve the goals open and flexible. The state standards require Ms. Stevens's students to demonstrate competency in persuasive writing. Using the standards, she sets a clear learning goal of mastering persuasive writing, but varies the practices that she uses to help them achieve it. She begins the unit by providing whole-class instruction in constructing an argument. Once students demonstrate that they understand and can formulate their own arguments, she sets up the online discussion forum to give them more independent practice with feedback. She monitors forum participation very closely, and she frequently confers with individual students while the rest of the class works independently.

LEARNING PERSUASIVE WRITING BY USING AN ONLINE FORUM

Until now, many students have only been asked to identify or summarize main ideas in what they've read. Forming an argument requires them to take the next steps: to state their position on the main idea or problem they've identified, and to support their position with evidence. As a tool for online dialogue, a discussion forum can help students learn and practice composing arguments. In such a forum, the purpose for writing and the audience are both clearly established. Discussion threads are organized by topics, and students write to communicate directly with their peers and the teacher. Below are a few tips for using an online forum to support writing:

- Set aside time in class for students to post and to reply to their peers' posts.
- If Internet access outside school is not a barrier, assign a discussion in a forum as a homework assignment.
- Remind students to:
  - Focus on writing one clear idea per post.
  - Be respectful when disagreeing with what someone else has posted.
  - Recognize that their position on a topic need not be theirs forever. It can be intimidating for them to take a stand on an issue at times, especially when they put it in writing. It's okay for authors to change their minds.

DISCUSSION FORUM SOFTWARE

Google Groups

http://groups.google.com

Google has a free discussion-forum-hosting application called Google Groups. Users can set up a forum by following the steps provided on the site. Google Groups provide users with the option to create a public forum available for anyone to read and post, or a private forum that restricts access to students in a class.

Forumotion

http://www.forumotion.com

Forumotion also offers a free forum-hosting service similar to Google Groups.

Forum Software

http://www.forum-software.org

If a school or district is considering hosting its own discussion forum, this website has resources to help choose forum software that matches school or district needs. It has demos, reviews of different forum software applications, and a comparison tool for users to select and compare forum features across multiple applications.

The UDL strategies also recommend providing scaffolds for practice and performance, as well as opportunities to engage in a cycle of practice and reflection—that is, to try out new knowledge and skills and receive immediate feedback. Ms. Stevens structures the process for learning to write a persuasive essay into discrete, comprehensible, and achievable steps. She starts with a single element—constructing a good argument—and scaffolds the writing process by first modeling how to take apart a weak argument and then reconstruct it to make it stronger. No one has a perfect argument on the first try. But by having the whole class do the exercise, and providing multiple practices with feedback, Ms. Stevens instills in her students the value of revision. Later, the forum provides students with opportunities to practice giving and receiving feedback and making appropriate revisions.

WRITING TO LEARN ACROSS THE CURRICULUM: EAST HIGH SCHOOL

An unusual scene is unfolding at East High School. Nearly 50 students are packed into a large classroom. An inquisitive visitor peering through the window in the classroom door may notice the rich artifacts, documents, maps, and posters surrounding the crowded room, and conjecture that this must be a history class. But something doesn't quite fit. Why is every student paging through Mark Twain's *The Adventures of Huckleberry Finn*? Curious, the visitor may open the door slightly to eavesdrop on the invigorating discussion.

A student is describing a passage from the novel in which Jim, a slave, is sharing his plans to run away with Huck. Jim is much older than Huck, yet treats Huck as his senior. The student is using the characters' interaction to compare and contrast today's social mores with those of the antebellum South. Images from the antebellum South are projected on the SMART board in front of the class. Ms. Saunders shifts the conversation about the novel to focus on primary source materials available on the Internet. A webpage showing newspaper ads of slave holders calling for the return of runaway slaves is projected on the board. As a hook to engage students, she strategically selects a "want ad" from a listing written by a famous revolutionary, Thomas Jefferson. He had placed an ad offering a reward for the return of his slave. Not surprisingly, the image sparks a lively discussion among students over the fact that Jefferson—the author of the Declaration of Independence, and a President of the United States—had slaves!

Most people think of writing instruction as something that happens exclusively in ELA class. In fact, writing instruction can—and by all accounts should—take place across the curriculum, providing opportunities for greater engagement and practice in a purposeful context. In this case, Ms. Saunders, an ELA teacher, and Mr. Drew, a history teacher, have combined their classes to blend ELA with writing instruction and U.S. history lessons.

In the past, Ms. Saunders would have spent a class period or more providing background knowledge so that her students would have a historical, social, and vernacular context to make sense of *Huckleberry Finn*. Similarly, Mr. Drew would have wrestled with how to help his students express what they learned about history in readable prose. Now both teachers are sharing the responsibility to teach writing and help students learn about the antebellum South. The interdisciplinary collaboration enables these teachers to leverage each other's interest and expertise, as well as to pique students' interest in literature and historical contexts. Students develop critical thinking skills through literary analysis of the novel and further hone those skills by analyzing primary sources in history. Students are graded for both historical accuracy and writing ability. Best of all, students' knowledge and skills are improving, and learning has become more meaningful and engaging. Students' motivation, energy, and enthusiasm for reading American literature and learning U.S. history are growing.

Using UDL Strategies for Teaching Writing across the Curriculum

Effective teaching and learning start with setting clear goals (the first of the UDL strategiess for teaching writing). Looking broadly across their curriculum, and specifically at their two content areas, Ms. Saunders and Mr. Drew identified overlapping knowledge and skills that students must acquire. They saw writing, critical thinking, and learning as interconnected skills, and they focused on writing to learn as an integral part of both content areas. This enabled them to think creatively and strategically about how to distribute teaching responsibilities and make the best use of each other's skills and expertise. Ms. Saunders now supports students in developing a literary lens. In the *Huckleberry Finn* unit, for example, students learn to view and understand the antebellum South from the perspective of characters in the novel. Correspondingly, Mr. Drew now helps students in developing a historical lens—in the case of *Huckleberry Finn*, through analyzing primary sources from the antebellum period. Students review primary sources stored in a digital library on the Internet and examine physical artifacts in the classrooms. Ms. Saunders teaches the process of writing. And Mr. Drew emphasizes the importance of writing as a learning strategy by teaching students how to think and write for history. Co-teaching enables both of them to vary the challenges and supports necessary to create an optimal learning environment. Their students learn to write and to apply writing skills in the service of learning in both disciplines.

Writing is also difficult and demanding for both novice and experienced writers. Another effective UDL strategy for engaging learners and sustaining motivation to write is to provide choices of topics and means for composing. Co-teaching helps Ms. Saunders and Mr. Drew to design interdisciplinary lessons that weave together literature, history, and students' interest in and knowledge of popular culture. Their interdisciplinary assignments make writing an integral component of how both ELA and history are taught. As a result, students feel more invested in learning. Students draw upon their background knowledge and expertise, and write about *Huckleberry Finn* and the topics of other units from angles that are meaningful to them.

WRITING TO LEARN ACROSS THE CURRICULUM

The teachers in the East High School example of UDL co-teaching illustrate pedagogical efficiencies for multiple instructional goals for high school students. These teachers—and for that matter, schools, society, and standards—value writing. As a result, they have determined that a focus on writing across ELA and history is a legitimate way to facilitate learning and thinking for each content area. Here are some of the strategies Mr. Drew and Ms. Saunders have incorporated into their co-teaching instructional design:

- The curriculum goals for ELA and history each require substantial prior knowledge. Teachers cannot make assumptions about students' background knowledge in either context and must "preteach" for maximum understanding.
- These teachers realize that not all history and ELA topic areas are interesting to every student. Yet, to meet instructional goals, engagement is essential. For the *Huckleberry Finn* unit, they have enlisted several techniques to maximize student interest and enhance instruction: (1) making connections between historic events and current events; (2) using primary source documents from famous people (e.g., Thomas Jefferson); and (3) providing choices of topic and structure in writing assignments.
- Many readings in both history and ELA use language structures that are unlike our current and common English usage. To provide supports for *Huckleberry Finn*, the teachers frequently have passages read aloud in class; they then overtly discuss what uncommon or out-of-date words or phrases mean, and literally "translate" the older English into modern, understandable language.

PRACTICES AND BENEFITS OF FORMATIVE ASSESSMENT

When teachers are assessing writing, it is important to select assessment practices that are aligned with the learning goals. In writing instruction, the learning goal is to help novice learners develop into proficient writers. Mastering the writing process is important to producing a high-quality essay. Accordingly, assessment data should be used to improve the students' learning process (Graham, Harris, & Hebert, 2011). In the first two case examples presented above, three styles of "formative assessment" are illustrated: progress monitoring, peer assessment, and self-assessment. They share a common goal—the direct assessment of student writing by both students and teachers for the purpose of supporting, guiding, and monitoring the students' learning process. Involving students in the act of assessment produces better writing (Amato & Watkins, 2011; Murphy & Yancey, 2008; Topping, 2009). The following is a short description of each type of formative assessment, its practice, and its benefits.

"Progress monitoring" is a system of frequently administered assessments that provide data to inform instructional adjustments. When such assessments are tied directly to the curriculum, the process is known as "curriculum-based measurement" (CBM). CBM is a valid and reliable progress-monitoring system that allows teachers to evaluate the effects of their writing interventions for their students. When interventions are not effective, teachers can modify interventions, and then further evaluate those modifications. This type of progress monitoring is built into MassONE Writer, the topic of the first case example in this chapter.

The progress-monitoring feature of MassONE Writer enables a teacher to assign a writing task to students at a regular interval (twice a month). Students use the built-in word editor to complete the writing task. Then the teacher evaluates student writing for content, cohesion, coherence, and mechanics (spelling, grammar, etc.), and uses an annotation tool to mark errors and add comments. The teacher can then arrange one-to-one conferences with students to review their writing. Together, they can discuss growth in different areas of writing: content, style, flow, completeness, and mechanics of writing. The teacher can also use these data to make decisions about writing instruction for students on both a group and an individual basis. The teacher may modify instruction for students, provide practice, and then follow up with additional progress monitoring to evaluate whether the intervention or modified instruction improves students' writing performance. MassONE Writer thus seamlessly integrates writing tools, scaffolds and supports for writing instruction, and progress monitoring.

"Peer assessment" is an ongoing activity that is arranged reciprocally between the assessors and the assessed. Teachers guide and co-create with students the criteria for evaluating student writing. They discuss strategies for providing meaningful feedback. Students apply the criteria to evaluate and provide feedback on their classmates' writing. Active student participation in all phases of peer assessment results in deeper understanding of writing and deeper engagement by students throughout the writing process (Topping, 2009). Finally, frequent, precise, and constructive feedback from teachers and peers leads to substantial gains in writing skills (Murphy & Yancey, 2008).

"Self-assessment" is similar to peer assessment, in that teachers and students co-create criteria for assessing writing and discuss strategies for giving feedback. The difference is that self-assessment is a reflective process in which students make meaning of their peers' and teachers' feedback and critique their own writing. Self-assessment encourages students to evaluate, monitor, and reflect on their own performance (Murphy & Yancey, 2008).

As described above in "Learning Persuasive Writing: JFK Middle School," peer and self-assessments are integral to learning the writing process. To begin with, Ms. Stevens stirs up controversy by tightening classroom rules and stripping away student privileges. This primes students for a lesson on argumentation. As the scenario unfolds, students and teacher negotiate and co-construct a definition of an argument, determine the criteria for evaluating arguments, and practice constructing effective arguments and using feedback from peers. The iterative writing and peer assessment practice start as a class discussion and then continue into an online discussion forum where students respond to each other's posts from different perspectives. Later, students apply their writing and argument building strategies to academic persuasive essays. Peer assessment helps these students evaluate and provide feedback on each other's writing, and self-assessment helps them to evaluate and revise their own writing. Students' authentic involvement in the writing and assessment process from the very beginning result in deeper understanding of the writing process and in better essays.

DEVELOPING WRITERS WHO WRITE WELL—AND OFTEN

Today, the focus on improving student writing scores to meet competency standards risks inadvertently turning teachers into technicians who are skilled at preparing students to write for large-scale assessments, instead of imparting the knowledge and skills students need to use writing to think, learn, and participate across different situations. Current writing curricula, instructional practice, and teacher training need to take advantage of what we know about learners, effective writing instruction, and web-based technology. Learners differ in the ways they access and understand information, express knowledge and skills, and are engaged and motivated to write. Writing is a skill that is not easily transferred across different forms and content areas. Students who have learned how to write in one form or discipline may not always write as competently in other forms and disciplines. Students need direct instruction on how to write and think in each discipline, and opportunities to practice writing and emulating models of good writing for each field. Setting high expectations without providing flexible means and appropriate supports will only increase students' anxiety and fear of writing.

The UDL framework can guide educators to design learning strategies that weave together effective writing models and web-based technology to meet the needs of diverse learners. UDL strategies help educators to set clear goals, to provide flexible means of achieving them, and to instill in students the desire to write well and often.

REFERENCES

Amato, J. M., & Watkins, M. W. (2011). The predictive validity of CBM writing indices for eighth-grade students. *Journal of Special Education, 44,* 195–204.

Applebee, A., & Langer, J. (2006). *The state of writing instruction: What existing data tell us.* Albany, NY: Center on English Learning and Achievement.

CAST. (2011). *Universal Design for Learning Guidelines version 2.0.* Wakefield, MA: Author. Retrieved from *http://www.udlcenter.org/aboutudl/udlguidelines.*

College Board. (2008). *SAT writing section.* Retrieved from *http://www.collegeboard.com/student/testing/sat/about/sat/writing.html.*

Gabriel, R. (2002). *Writers' workshops and the work of making things.* New York: Addison Wesley Longman.

Gersten, R., & Baker, S. (2001). Teaching expressive writing to students with learning disabilities: A meta-analysis. *Elementary School Journal, 101*(3), 251–272.

Graham, S., & Harris, K. (2000). The role of self-regulation and transcription skills in writing and writing development. *Educational Psychologist, 1,* 3–12.

Graham, S., Harris, K., & Hebert, M. (2011). *Informing writing: The benefits of formative assessment* (A report to Carnegie Corporation of New York). New York: Alliance for Excellence in Education.

Graham, S., MacArthur, C. A., & Fitzgerald, J. (Eds.). (2007). *Best practices in writing instruction.* New York: Guilford Press.

Graham, S., & Perin, D. (2007). *Writing next: Effective strategies to improve writing of adolescents in middle and high schools* (A report to Carnegie Corporation of New York). New York: Alliance for Excellence in Education.

Johnson, L. F., Levine, A., Smith, R. S., & Stone, S. (2010). *2010 Horizon Report.* Austin, TX: New Media Consortium.

Langer, J. A. (2009). Contexts for adolescent literacy. In L. Christenbury, R. Bomer, & P. Smagorinsky (Eds.), *Handbook of adolescent literacy research* (pp. 49–64). New York: Guilford Press.

McKee, R. (1997). *Story: Substance, structure, style and the principles of screenwriting.* New York: HarperCollins.

Murphy, S., & Yancey, K.B. (2008). Construct and consequence: Validity in writing assessment. In C. Bazerman (Ed.), *Handbook of research on writing: History, society, school, individual, text* (pp. 448–474). New York: Erlbaum.

National Center for Education Statistics. (2008). *The nation's report card: Writing. Percentage of students by writing achievement level.* Retrieved from *http://nces.ed.gov/nationsreportcard/ pdf/main2007/2008468.pdf.*

Olson, C. B. (2011). *The reading/writing connection: Strategies for teaching and learning in the secondary classroom* (3rd ed.). Boston: Pearson.

Stein, M., Dixon, R., & Barnard, S. (2001). What research tells us about writing instruction for students in the middle grades. *Journal of Direct Instruction, 1*(2), 107–116.

Topping, K. J. (2009). Peer assessment. *Theory into Practice, 48,* 20–27.

Zinsser, W. (1988). *Writing to learn.* New York: Harper & Row.

CHAPTER 5

Universal Design for Learning in the Science Classroom

JEREMY FOREST PRICE, MINDY JOHNSON, and MICHAEL BARNETT

Understanding and engaging with scientific language, concepts, and consequences are becoming much more important aspects of what it means to be an educated person, an informed and active citizen, and a successful worker, as well as a knowledgeable and critical consumer. The National Academy of Sciences' *Taking Science to School* report (Duschl, Schweingruber, & Shouse, 2007) provides a very good description of what a successful educational experience in science might look like, in the form of four intertwined and interrelated strands. Ideally, these strands of science education should constitute what is widely expected of learners in the science classroom. According to this report, "learning" science is as much about "using," "interpreting," and "participating" as it is about "knowing" science. This approach opens the field of science learning up for a wide range of individuals who may thrive in a science-learning environment that is hands-on and connected to direct experience.

A number of skills, attitudes, and knowledge sets are still required for successful engagement in science class, especially within this approach. It is those students "in the margins"—those students whose abilities or disabilities, or whose linguistic, cultural, and experiential backgrounds, do not fit the profile of what we consider "easy" students to reach—who are most easily frustrated with and most often left out in the science classroom. Using the practical Guidelines of Universal Design for Learning (UDL) in conjunction with a judicious use of technology can help provide a supportive learning environment that allows successful inclusion of a diversity of students, especially those students in the margins.

This chapter explores some potential barriers that students with a range of abilities and experiences may face in engaging with science in the classroom. We describe ways in which the use of technology, together with consideration of the UDL Guidelines, can provide opportunities for a diversity of learners to engage deeply and successfully with science in the classroom. We also describe the ways in which the assessment of science learning is affected by the UDL-driven use of technology, as well as ways to consider using technology outside the classroom, such as at home, outdoors, or in museums.

POTENTIAL BARRIERS TO SCIENCE LEARNING

In order to discuss the potential barriers that students with a range of abilities–disabilities, experiences, and background knowledge may face in learning science, we describe some of the processes, skills, and knowledge necessary to fulfill the high standards of participation in the scientific enterprise. Thinking not about what needs to be conveyed or practiced in order to teach science, but instead thinking about what students experience when they learn science, we propose the following three types of learning activities in science (see Table 5.1).

Thinking in Science

Learning and participating in science require particular ways of thinking and analyzing information in order to make meaning and sense of the world. This strand includes some of the "habits of mind," or ways of thinking, that students are expected to acquire to succeed in the science classroom (Lee & Fradd, 1998). These habits of mind frequently differ from "common sense." Scientific inquiry itself can provide a completely open and disorienting experience, even when there are outcomes that should be consistent with scientific consensus (Donnelly, 2002), and can therefore be a barrier to a range of students.

**TABLE 5.1. Potential Barriers to Learning Science:
Requirements of the Scientific Enterprise**

Thinking in science
- "Scientific" approach (versus "common-sense" approach)
- Open-ended inquiry

Talking in science
- Receiving, interpreting, and expressing knowledge about the world through numbers
- Understanding and creating by using the vocabulary and structure of science

Doing in science
- Following scientific protocols
- Collaborating in science

A Student Example

A sixth-grade girl is writing a lab report for an experiment about the validity of the home field advantage for sports teams. The student follows 10 baseball teams over the course of a season, collecting the scores for all of the games. The data suggest that, despite the fact that some teams do seem to win more games at home, in general there is no home field advantage over the course of the season; on average, just as many games are won and lost at home. The student, however, concludes that because a few teams do win more games at home, her hypothesis has been upheld; she still believes that there is a home field advantage for baseball teams. The popular cultural belief of the home field advantage has influenced the student's interpretation of her findings. She cannot separate her preconception of a home field advantage from the data she has collected and analyzed. Because some of the results support her preconception, she feels that her interpretation has been validated.

Talking in Science

Besides the "habits of mind" that are important to science learning, students are expected to be able to (in some senses) "talk like a scientist." This involves being able to express ideas and data that "sound like" and "look like" science. Most frequently, this involves working with numbers and creating charts, graphs, and reports. This can be a new, difficult, and frustrating experience for a range of students.

A Student Example

A ninth-grade student is required to create a human population growth graph on paper, using a data table with population estimates from the year 1800 to 2008. The student is then asked to extrapolate data to the year 2025. The data given are sporadic; early decades are skipped, although there is yearly information for the years 1960 through 2008. The student, instead of using equal intervals to number the axes, uses just the given years as points on the graph.

Though the student has made many graphs before in math class, using "real" data containing gaps and inconsistent information causes confusion. The student has trouble grasping the concept that these numbers represent periods of time and numbers of people. Also, because the numbers are so large (the extrapolation of the graph requires that the Y-axis go to 10 billion at least), creating a scale and intervals with these unfamiliar numbers (e.g., 1,000 million = 1 billion) becomes an incredibly abstract task.

Doing in Science

Lastly, science is not just about thinking, but also about doing—experimenting, collecting, and building. The doing, such as in lab exercises, frequently involves using a particular set of methods and following a particular protocol. To various students, the instructions and protocols for these exercises provide a bewildering array of steps that may be too dense, too detailed, or not detailed enough. In addition, because of the various benefits to collaborative learning, lab exercises are often done in pairs or groups. This group configuration, in turn, has the potential to create barriers.

A Student Example

A third-grade boy is asked to test a variety of given objects to see whether they stick to a magnet. The objects include a rubber band, a shiny nail (aluminum), a dull nail (steel), a paper clip, a black rock (magnetite), and a grey rock (sandstone). At the end of the activity, the student is asked to make a rule about what sticks to magnets. At first, the student makes predictions that the two nails and the paper clip will stick to the magnet; he is most likely working on the assumption that metal objects stick to magnets.

After the experiment, the student is left with confusing data that do not match his predictions. Of the two nails, only the steel nail sticks to the magnet, and of the rocks, the black one sticks to the magnet. The teacher goes over what each of the materials is made of, but the student is left using his confusing data to make his rule about what sticks to magnets. Though the student has followed the inquiry activity as the teacher intended, he has difficulty noticing the similarities between the objects that stick to magnets, and is challenged even further by the idea of generalizing a rule based on his data.

ADDRESSING BARRIERS IN THE SCIENCE CLASSROOM WITH UDL AND TECHNOLOGY

Technology in the classroom—when designed and used with UDL in mind—can provide students and teachers with powerful opportunities to minimize or overcome the barriers described above. It is worth repeating here that a fundamental concept underlying UDL is that there is, and always will be, a diversity of students with a variety of experiences, strengths, weaknesses, interests, and backgrounds. Technology, in conjunction with a good curriculum and effective supportive teaching, can provide flexibility in the materials, goals, methods, and assessments. This flexibility can provide students opportunities to learn and succeed along their own pathways and at their own pace while maintaining high standards and expectations for all.

The UDL Guidelines (CAST, 2011) provide educators and curriculum developers with a strategic framework for designing and developing materials, goals, methods, and assessments, as well as using these components of instruction. As described in detail by Lapinski, Gravel, and Rose in Chapter 2 of this book, the UDL Guidelines are organized along the three principles of UDL, addressing representation, action/expression, and engagement.

The three types of learning activities described in this chapter—thinking in science, talking in science, and doing in science—each incorporate aspects of these principles. For example, completing a lab exercise is a standard doing-in-science activity. First, it requires a teacher to consider the representation of the materials (in terms of providing scaffolding and supports to complement any written instructions, and determining how those instructions are written), as well as to consider any other representations of data students may encounter in the lab (chemical color changes, smells, etc.). These all pertain to Principle I of UDL.

A lab exercise also requires considering each student's opportunities for action and expression (Principle II of UDL), such as how he or she will interact with the materials, follow the required steps, and record and report the data and findings. Lastly, a lab exercise also requires considering the quality of the student's engagement (Principle III of UDL), such as what makes the exercise an important part of the science curriculum, its relevance for the student's life, and the implications for mastery and the student's identity as a learner (engagement). Table 5.2 shows the three types of science-learning activities, along with useful checkpoints from the UDL Guidelines.

TABLE 5.2. Addressing Barriers in the Science Classroom with UDL and Technology

	Scaffolding for representation	Scaffolding for action and expression	Scaffolding for engagement
Thinking in science		• Modeling scientific thinking and inquiry • Activating background knowledge and experience • Opportunities to compare and contrast "thinking in science" with "everyday thinking"	• Valuing students' preconceptions as opportunities for growth rather than as things to replace
Talking in science	• Vocabulary supports • Highlighting key concepts and embedding guiding questions for text, charts, and graphs • Availability of screen reader	• Simulations to develop numerical literacies • Providing document structure and scaffolding for scientific report writing • Providing opportunities to express scientific knowledge by using multimedia	• Providing opportunities for critical science agency and community involvement
Doing in science	• Breaking lengthy instructions into manageable tasks • Providing video or photographic examples of tasks	• Using probeware to collect data • Distributing tasks among members of a group and sharing data and findings	• Connecting with everyday experiences and phenomena

Thinking in Science

As noted above, the science classroom requires that students think about and observe the world in a specific and methodological way. The scientist's objective view and approach to problem solving can come into conflict with (or at least seem extremely foreign to) the "default" approach for a diversity of students, because of experience or skills. Even though it is neither necessary nor even desired for every student to become a scientist or even harbor aspirations of a career in the sciences (although it is always exciting and promising when it happens!), science educators Munby and Roberts (1998) point to the necessity of students' mastering some level of "intellectual independence" to evaluate and investigate claims and phenomena in science. This requires students to be aware of this special way of thinking in science, and to be able to engage in such thinking in a productive and effective manner.

Being aware of the specialized way of thinking in science also means being able to compare and contrast the "science way" with the way that students typically engage and think about the natural world, and to engage these different ways in dialogue. Intellectual independence involves being able to do this on one's own, as well as knowing when to seek help in making these comparisons. Technology designed and used with UDL in mind can help students reach this independence by supplementing materials in the science classroom with appropriate scaffolding and supports.

Background Knowledge

The UDL Guidelines point to the importance of activating "background knowledge" when students are thinking in science. In the meaning-making process in science, it is important to help students find commonalities and connections with what they already cognitively and experientially "bring to the table." The same can be said for any school subject, but this task is especially difficult in science, given the discrepancies between thinking in science and the "everyday" way of thinking.

As a way to scaffold this process, it is important to help students see the connections between what they are learning in science and what they have already known or experienced, as mentioned above. It is also necessary to help students see where they are (in terms of what they know and how they think about the world), and what the expectations are in science class (in terms of understanding the world in a specific way).

Models and Simulations

Providing models or simulations of concepts that are typically misunderstood can help confront students' misconceptions head-on, providing a springboard for further discussion and enhanced understanding. CAST's Science Writer (*http://science-writer.cast.org*) provides students with online virtual avatars that serve as helpers or guides in the science inquiry process (Figure 5.1). These avatars model several

FIGURE 5.1. An example of an animated agent providing a model of his own scientific experiment in the Science Writer application (*http://sciencewriter.cast.org*). Copyright 2011 by CAST, Inc. All rights reserved. Used with permission.

different approaches to scientific problem solving, as well as prompting students to consider new ideas and new data in light of their past experiences and knowledge. This allows students to practice these skills, approaches, and ways of thinking about the world, and to model their attempts after the avatars' work.

Discussions

A teacher can also have discussions with individual students or the class as a whole about what was surprising or new for them in following the approaches modeled by the avatars, why the avatars' approaches model "good science," and how they may have been different from how the students would have approached the problem or inquiry on their own.

In considering the usefulness of discussion, it is also important to remember the distinction between "misconceptions" and "preconceptions" in these conversations. Students are not blank slates, and always cognitively and experientially bring something to the classroom. Physicist and educator Martin Eger (1992) reminds us that these preconceptions are important and natural starting points for students to expand their knowledge and understanding of science concepts and phenomena. They are not necessarily misconceptions, or inbred and stubborn mistakes to replace or correct; instead, these preconceptions are opportunities for growth, development, and deepened understanding of science, the scientific way of thinking, and scientific concepts and natural phenomena. Preconceptions need to be treated with respect, in order to help foster an engaging and safe inclusive learning environment in the science classroom.

The student in the first example presented earlier, who is having trouble discriminating between scientifically collected and analyzed data and her own experience, could benefit from a discussion about the difference between these two ways of developing knowledge and conclusions. Providing an authentic model of the method used for the scientific inquiry, along with think-aloud modeling of working through the processes, could support the student in understanding the difference between scientific thinking and experiential thinking.

Talking in Science

Text-Based Communication (Reading)

Talking in science is not just expressing oneself verbally in a scientific manner. It is being able to engage in the full range of communicative activities in science, including reading, writing, negotiating, and, yes, talking. As noted above, science requires that learners pick up a great deal of specialized vocabulary. Digital texts potentially have the flexibility to provide embedded and on-demand vocabulary-based scaffolding, which provide not only textual definitions but also photographs and diagrams (Figure 5.2). This form of scaffolding can also provide examples and nonexamples of a phenomenon or concept, in order to help students understand its conceptual boundaries. Providing materials in the appropriate digital format allows students to use screen readers for decoding support as they read, as well as allowing students to use refreshable Braille devices, to display the text in a large format, or to display it in any necessary color combination. This adaptability in instructional materials enables teachers to provide an individualized format that allows students to focus on the meaning of the text.

The UrbanEcoLab, an online, interactive high-school-level urban ecology curriculum,[1] provides students with these embedded and on-demand vocabulary scaffolds within texts. Students are able to click on each key word and read its definition, see a diagram or photo illustrating the word, and see examples and nonexamples of the word. Students are also provided with the option to have key concepts highlighted for them, helping them pick out the important parts of the text. As they become better readers in science texts and more efficient at recognizing key concepts, students do not need these forms of scaffolding and rely on them less and less.

CAST's UDL Book Builder (*http://bookbuilder.cast.org*) provides teachers with the ability to create online texts with images for their students. These texts are presented in well-formed HTML, facilitating the use of embedded screen readers for students who benefit from them. In addition, teachers can easily create embedded supports and scaffolding, such as vocabulary supports, audio enhancements, and animated agents to provide students with peer-like interactive models, hints, and strategies. Students may also use the UDL Book Builder to complete assignments and organize them in a portfolio-like manner. The Book Builder Public Library contains thousands of teacher- and student-created books that others can use in their classrooms immediately.

In addition to online texts already available for use in the classroom—for example, the University of Wisconsin's The Why Files (*http://www.whyfiles.org*) is a wonderful resource for finding useful articles on the "science behind the news"—teachers

---

[1] Developed by Boston College, the Urban Ecology Institute, and CAST, the UrbanEcoLab is a UDL-based version of the curriculum UrbanEcoLab: How Do We Develop Healthy Cities?, funded by the National Science Foundation (Grant No. 0607010).

FIGURE 5.2. A reading passage from UrbanEcoLab, with key concepts highlighted and the term "hazardous substances" defined within the context of the surrounding text. Students can activate these forms of scaffolding as needed. Copyright 2011 by CAST, Inc. All rights reserved. Used with permission.

ENGAGING STUDENTS IN SCIENCE

As mentioned many times in this chapter, allowing students to find connections between science and their everyday lives and experiences is important for helping them learn and make sense of science, as well as for helping many students to find science interesting and relevant. Science educator Angela Calabrese Barton (2002) recommends that one goal of science education, especially for urban classrooms, should be providing students with opportunities for "critical science agency." That is, science should be seen as a way for students to engage with their communities and neighborhoods, and to address issues and problems that have a scientific component (see also Hashimoto-Martell, McNeill, & Hoffman, 2011). For these ends, technology can be used in a variety of different ways to support this form of engagement:

- Research the news and issues of the community, as well as to find communities who may have similar stories.
- Connect with community members and institutions involved with the issues from the classroom over email or video conferencing, in conjunction with in-person visits.
- Connect with scientists who have experience in this area of science and/or public engagement over email or video conferencing.
- Draft and publish plans for engagement, and facilitate the collection of feedback from a variety of stakeholders, in the form of a blog or wiki.

Of course, this list is not exhaustive. In addition, teachers need to be aware that using technology for purposes of inclusion can be a double-edged sword: It can serve as an amazing and effective enabler and motivator for a large number of students, or it can exacerbate existing disabilities or create new "disabilities" that hadn't been noticed before.

If teachers require funding to purchase necessary technology equipment, the website DonorsChoose (*http://www.donorschoose.org*) allows them to post proposals for classroom projects that require funding, and donors from around the country and around the world can donate the funds. See the website for more information.

can use a webpage annotator, such as Diigo (*http://www.diigo.com*). Diigo provides free accounts to teachers, along with free, special, protected, nonpublic student accounts that are connected to a classroom and do not require an email address. Diigo allows teachers to highlight critical points on any HTML webpage to share with class, as well as to attach sticky notes to these highlights to provide students with a definition for a word or concept, or to provide them with a guiding question for them to consider this word or concept more deeply or in a different context. Diigo also allows for conversations to occur within these sticky notes, so that a teacher can ask a question about a particular point in the text and students can respond (Figure 5.3).

Text-Based Communication (Writing)

Technology designed with UDL in mind can also provide supported writing environments for writing scientific or lab reports, as well as keeping track of and organizing observations. CAST's Science Writer (*http://sciencewriter.cast.org*) provides scaffolding and modeling not only for approaching science inquiry, but also for writing reports. Students are provided with scaffolding in the form of a standard document structure (introduction/thesis, methods/procedures, results, and conclusion/discussion), as well as hints, tips, and the continued presence of the online animated avatars to model the process along the way. Students can approach this structure one section at a time to help them focus on a particular set of thinking and writing skills, or students may write a report all at once. Students are also encouraged to follow a revision/editing process to polish their writing as they work through the sections of the report.

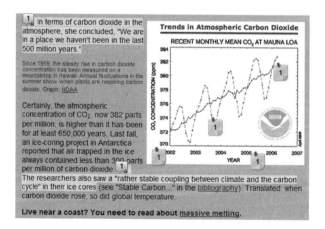

FIGURE 5.3. An example of the Web annotation tool Diigo in action on The Why Files' "Blue Earth Day" page (*http://whyfiles.org/238earthday/index.php?g=1.txt*). Note the digital "sticky notes" that point out critical features, as well as highlighting within the text to indicate a critical point of information. Content copyright 2012 by University of Wisconsin Board of Regents. Diigo annotations software copyright 2012 by Diigo, Inc. All rights reserved. Used with permission.

Numerical Communication

Scientific communication is done not only in text, but also to a great degree in numbers. Students are expected to read, interpret, and create tables, charts, and graphs. As this may be a new and difficult experience for a range of students, technology with UDL in mind can provide a great deal of just-in-time and embedded support. UDL-designed technology can also provide a structure for creating charts and graphs, leading those students who need it through a step-by-step procedure until they become more practiced, experienced, skilled, and comfortable at creating these.

Students with physical disabilities, visual disabilities, or fine motor or motor planning difficulties can have an extremely difficult time with the skills required to create graphs on paper. Computer-assisted graphing tools are essential for these students; without these tools, students cannot fully participate in the activity. Online graphing materials and programs available on the web, such as the free Create A Graph (*http://nces.ed.gov/nceskids/createagraph*), can be enhanced with Diigo. Diigo allows a teacher to place a free-floating sticky note anywhere on a page, including on top of images and graphs. This feature allows the teacher to point out the various universal traits of graphs, such as axes, scales, and titles, as well as to point out critical trends in a graph that are necessary for understanding what the graph is trying to say. Again, these features are on demand, and can be used or not. As students become more skilled at reading and understanding graphs, they will need these embedded scaffolds less and less.

Simulations are another technology-supported way to help students communicate in science with numbers. A computer-based simulation provides students with an alternative graphical and dynamic representation of the underlying numerical structure and data. Students have the ability to manipulate variables, such as numbers of predators or prey, and get immediate feedback. The Concord Consortium (*http://www.concord.org*) provides a number of high-quality simulation and visual modeling software programs in a number of science-related fields. Keep in mind, however, that many students may need some help, especially at the beginning, in making connections between icons and colors on the screen and the underlying numbers and structures. Also, because science can provide a number of wonderful hands-on experiences, it is important to complement these technology-facilitated experiences with ones where students get their hands dirty (figuratively or literally) in exploring the world around them. These can take place in the laboratory, on the school grounds, or in a local park.

Multimedia Communication

Approaching technology with UDL as a framework also allows teachers to provide students with multimedia tools to express themselves and their scientific understandings. For instance, technology makes producing a video, animation, or audio clip fairly easy and places it within reach of teachers and students. Both Macs and

PCs come with bundled software for creating video (Apple's iLife and Windows Movie Maker, respectively), and they are easy to use.

In addition, comics are an engaging and sophisticated medium for communicating information. The National Council of Teachers of English and the International Reading Association provide a free online ComicCreator (*http://www.readwritethink. org/classroom-resources/student-interactives/comic-creator-30021.html*); Plasq offers the software Comic Life (*http://plasq.com*), which is not free but is more feature-rich.

Although the skills and knowledge necessary to communicate in and interpret traditional modes of science (e.g., the lab report) are of the utmost importance, multimedia may help provide an engaging bridge for many students into science, by helping them to build their confidence and basic understandings of the underlying science concepts and principles. In addition, these nontraditional models of science communication are useful in conveying complex scientific concepts to the larger public—a skill that is becoming more important to scientists and nonscientists alike.

Doing in Science

Doing in science—that is, carrying out the activities expected in the science classroom—can be a dizzying and frustrating experience. An activity is often completed by a group, and the students are expected to record their observations in real time. For a range of students, this process, without appropriate scaffolding, can pose a great challenge. Technology designed with UDL in mind, however, can provide some important ways for students to meet and overcome these barriers. Through these steps, it is important to remind students of how these activities can connect with their past experiences or the outside world. Otherwise, labs and other exercises may just be seen as tasks and activities to get through for school.

For example, technology can help offload some of the cognitive and physical energy required for keeping track of data. Probeware, such as the Concord Consortium's CCProbeware (*http://www.concord.org/research/probeware*) or a number of similar applications available for different handheld computer devices, allow students to connect probes such as thermometers to handheld devices. The software will track changes (e.g., in temperature) in real time as conditions change or as students try out the probes in new surroundings. Students can then go back and insert notes about the variables they have manipulated. This frees a range of students from the task of manually writing down data rapidly, and instead allows them to focus on the underlying questions and data analysis.

In addition, the emerging social nature of technology allows people to share information and data that will help students carry out exercises and experiments in the science classroom without overloading them, and thus will help them focus on actual science learning. Tasks can be split up by students within a lab group, as is frequently done, but the data entry only needs to be done once. Using something like the Google Docs Spreadsheet (*http://docs.google.com*) or Zoho Sheet (*http:// sheet.zoho.com*) can be one way to make use of freely available online applications.

TECHNOLOGY, UDL, AND SCIENCE OUTSIDE THE CLASSROOM

Science as a topic for learning and discussion can be found in great abundance outside the classroom. In fact, the potential for connecting with this wealth of resources and experiences can help make science learning interesting, fun, relevant, and important. Science can be found in students' backyards, on school grounds, in a local park, or in a science or natural history museum. Finding online resources for identifying plants, birds, and animals can be a great way to connect parents and children around science. Participating in a number of technology-facilitated "citizen scientist" initiatives, such as tracking bird populations or weather patterns, is also a great way of introducing children to science and the importance of learning science.

In addition, many scientists in museums and universities maintain blogs, so sending in questions via email or as video or sound files is a potentially exciting and confidence-building activity for any child, although especially for one who is marginalized because of ability, language, experience, or culture. In addition, many museums provide extensive resources on their websites, as well as information about their exhibits. A teacher will find it worthwhile to sit down with students and plan a visit together. Museums may also provide technology-based services (specialized to meet the needs of visitors with disabilities or not) that may help provide a better experience for students, such as audio tours, guiding questions for discussion, hands-on and technology-based exhibits with scaffolding and supports built-in, and customized tours based on students' interests and needs.

CAST's UDL Science Notebook (*http://cast.org/research/projects/snudl.html*), funded by ther Institute of Education Sciences recently pilot-tested in elementary classrooms, employs a feature to help facilitate this group work and data collection in classrooms where computer access and/or space is limited or group data collection is preferred. When the group data collection or note taking is complete, a student clicks the "group work" button and chooses the prepopulated names of the students in the group. The work is automatically sent to the selected students' notebooks. Students can then add their own revisions or additions, as the shared page is now part of each student's individual notebook.

The instructions for an activity or exercise are also frequently presented to students as a long list, which may be confusing to students who have difficulty reading long blocks of text or following long lists of instructions (such as those students executive function disabilities). Breaking up the instructions into manageable chunks and steps is always a good idea, but technology-based displays can also help students choose which display of instructions they prefer: a long list or a chunked list. Lastly, if instructions are rendered by using a tool such as CAST's UDL Book Builder (*http://bookbuilder.cast.org*), the same vocabulary and concept scaffolds can be embedded in the instructions for the activity, including scaffolding for students who may need prompting on when and how to interact with others in their group. A teacher can also embed photos or videos of these steps and tasks being carried out, especially complex or time-sensitive ones, in order to provide a form of modeling for students.

IMPLICATIONS FOR ASSESSMENT

Common criticisms of traditional assessments are that they are detached from instruction and practice, are not that informative about the evolution of a student's learning over time, and often are not designed to take into account the needs of a particular learner. Web-based and other digital technologies can enable all assessments to be dynamic and universally designed for the purpose of gathering information about students' understanding of not only scientific content, but also scientific processes. This latter aspect of assessment is particularly important in science, because most standards refer to the strong integration of scientific process and content.

One of the advantages of electronic media is that students can be assessed in a variety of ways, both explicitly and through embedded assessments. The latter are particularly attractive, because they provide detailed information without taking away from instructional time. For example, the Concord Consortium has been developing a series of virtual lab experiments for the elementary grades, in which students manipulate and collect real-world data to demonstrate their understanding of processes, methods, and outcomes. For example, as a part of its UDL project (*http://www.concord.org/projects/udl*), the Concord Consortium has students use probeware to collect real data, and the data are then displayed on a "smart graph." A smart graph allows students to dissect elements of the graph for greater reflection and deeper understanding. Interpreting a graph can be challenging for students, particularly elementary-age students; however, embedding scaffolds and tests for understanding within the graph provides students with instant feedback on whether their interpretation of the graph is correct.

Concord's work is not limited to smart graphing. It also provides avenues for students to express their ideas and thoughts through multiple means. For example, students are also provided with scaffolded assistance to questions and offered choices for demonstrating what they have learned through text or drawings (see Figure 5.4). In this way, students are supported through the entire scientific inquiry process, from data collection to data representation and interpretation; moreover, the assessment of learning does not occur only at the end of the process, but is embedded throughout their investigation.

Equally important, however, is giving teachers easy access to the results of student work. In the Concord Consortium's program, a Web portal permits teachers to monitor student progress on the basis of embedded assessments, and to change settings (amount of scaffolding) for each student accordingly. Furthermore, the results of the students' experiments and their ideas are monitored and summarized in a variety of interactive reports to teachers. The top-level report shows graphically what steps each student has completed. Teachers can drill down into these steps to see student work and send the students reactions. The same top-level view allows

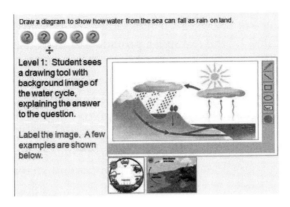

Draw a diagram to show how water from the sea can fall as rain on land.

Level 1: Student sees a drawing tool with background image of the water cycle, explaining the answer to the question.

Label the image. A few examples are shown below.

FIGURE 5.4. An example of using scaffolded assessment to gain a better understanding of a student's ideas about the water cycle. Content copyright 2012 by the Concord Consortium. Images copyright 2012 by Boulder Language Technologies. All rights reserved. Used with permission.

teachers to set the amount of scaffolding to provide to each student (see Figure 5.5). In particular, the teachers can easily track how the students use the materials, how much time they have spent on each task, and how much help or scaffolding the students have requested.

CONCLUSION

Technology, when used with UDL, can help provide an inclusive and supportive environment for students as they learn and grow in the science classroom. Students' development in thinking, talking, and doing in science can be fostered by considering the UDL principles of multiple modes of (I) representation, (II) student action and expression, and (III) engagement. Information and communication technology

Student Progress	Class Settings	Per Student Settings

	Activity 1	Activity 2	Activity 3	Activity 4	Scaffolding
John Smith	✔ ⊙▣	✔ ⊙▣	✔	Scaffolding ○ See all available	
Mary Fernandez	❶ ▣	✔ ⊙	✔	type ○ See one at a time	
Linh Dinn	⚠ ▣	⚠	✔ ▣		3 All
John Meyers	✔	✔	✔		3 1 by 1
Erika Vasquez	✔ ●	❶	✔ ●	Amount of	
Fermin Villegas	✔ ▣	⚠	✔ ▣	scaffolding	
Juan Torres	✔	✔	✔		5 All
Jose Toledo	✔	❶ ▣	⚠		5 All
Sam So	✔ ⊙	⚠ ▣	✔		4 All
Tamika Morris	⚠	✔	✔		2 1 by 1
LaShawn Brown	✔	✔ ●			2 1 by 1
Karen Smith	❶	✔ ▣			1 All
Clint Black	⚠	✔			5 All
Gene Hackman	✔	✔			4 All

FIGURE 5.5. Teacher page for changing the scaffolding settings. Copyright 2012 by the Concord Consortium. All rights reserved. Used with permission.

can have roles to play in providing this flexibility—and is already playing several such roles, as illustrated by the examples provided in this chapter. As the sciences become increasingly important aspects of our daily lives, activities, and political structures, it becomes even more important for all learners—regardless of ability, experience, or background—to be able to engage in and converse around the knowledge base and implications of the sciences. Technology and UDL can play an important part in this process.

Despite the use of technology to provide individualized scaffolding and support for students, teachers play a central and important role in the teaching and learning process in science. We certainly do not want to undersell the thoughtful judgment and necessary skills that teachers bring with them to the classroom each and every day. Teachers need to know their students as individuals—their needs, interests, and potentials—as well as to have a deep understanding of the subject matter and of how all these things interrelate and interact. UDL offers a framework for teachers to use technology in ways that help students grow and develop in our science-infused world.

REFERENCES

Calabrese Barton, A. (2002). Urban science education studies: A commitment to equity, social justice and a sense of place. *Studies in Science Education, 38*, 1–37.

CAST. (2011). *Universal Design for Learning Guidelines version 2.0.* Wakefield, MA: Author. Retrieved from *http://www.udlcenter.org/aboutudl/udlguidelines.*

Donnelly, J. F. (2002). Instrumentality, hermeneutics and the place of science in the school curriculum. *Science and Education, 11*(2), 135–153.

Duschl, R. A., Schweingruber, H. A., & Shouse, A. W. (Eds.). (2007). *Taking science to school: Learning and teaching science in grades K–8.* Washington, DC: National Academies Press.

Eger, M. (1992). Hermeneutics and science education: An introduction. *Science and Education, 1*(4), 337–348.

Hashimoto-Martell, E. A., McNeill, K. L., & Hoffman, E. M. (2011). Connecting urban youth with their environment: The impact of an urban ecology course on student content knowledge, environmental attitudes and responsible behaviors. *Research in Science Education.* Retrieved October 3, 2011, from *http://dx.doi.org/10.1007/s11165-011-9233-6.*

Lee, O., & Fradd, S. H. (1998). Science for all, including students from non-English-language backgrounds. *Educational Researcher, 27*(4), 12–21.

Munby, H., & Roberts, D. A. (1998). Intellectual independence: A potential link between science teaching and responsible citizenship. In D. A. Roberts & L. Östman (Eds.), *The problem of meaning in science curriculum* (pp. 101–114). New York: Teachers College Press.

CHAPTER 6

Universal Design for Learning in the Mathematics Classroom

ELIZABETH MURRAY and JACOB BROOKOVER

The stakes for achievement in mathematics have never been higher. Students who are successful in math in the secondary grades are more likely to be successful in college and to find high-quality employment after. Moreover, math is important in our everyday lives. We use it to manage our time and money, to understand data presented in the news, and to do tasks around the house (such as cooking or gardening). Yet many students struggle to learn math concepts, procedures, and facts. National and international assessments have highlighted the desperate need in the United States for more effective teaching and learning of mathematics at all grade levels.

In a research synthesis titled *Adding It Up*, a committee of the National Research Council described five attributes associated with proficiency in mathematics (National Research Council, 2001, p. 116):

1. Conceptual understanding (comprehension of mathematical concepts, operations, and relations—e.g., understanding that addition can be reversed through subtraction),
2. Procedural fluency (skills in carrying out procedures flexibly, fluently, and appropriately—e.g., solving a simple two-step algebraic equation, regardless of the numbers or variables in the problem).

3. Strategic competence (ability to formulate, represent, and solve mathematical problems—e.g., determining the minimum number of gallons of paint required to paint a room with several windows and doors).

4. Adaptive reasoning (capacity for logical thought, reflection, explanation, and justification—e.g., formulating and explaining a generalization for a pattern).

5. Productive disposition (habitual inclination to see mathematics as sensible, useful, and worthwhile, coupled with a belief in diligence and one's own efficacy).

These attributes can be classified according to the three brain networks that form the basis of the three principles of Universal Design for Learning (UDL). The first attribute is a function of recognition networks; the next three relate to strategic networks; and the last relates to the affective networks. We use these attributes to focus on barriers students face in learning mathematics.

MATH AND RECOGNITION NETWORKS

If students do not have a basic conceptual understanding of numbers, operations, patterns, and representations, they cannot fully grasp mathematics—even if they develop some skill in following the procedures they learn in school. Recognition networks play a major role in the development of conceptual knowledge, which involves the linking of these representations in meaningful ways (Dehaene, 1997; Hasselbring & Moore, 1996; Hiebert & Lefevre, 1986; Smith & Katz, 1996; Marshall, Superfine, & Canty, 2010; Thelen & Smith, 1994). Many components of mathematics rely on recognition networks. For example, students are expected to interpret and internalize models of numbers and operations. Recognizing spatial relations between objects is essential in many aspects of mathematics (van Garderen & Montague, 2003). Proficiency in algebra requires the ability to grasp the relationship between patterns in numbers and functions that represent them (Brown & Mehilos, 2010; National Council of Teachers of Mathematics [NCTM], 1998, 2000). In addition, conceptual understanding of mathematics is enhanced when learners have the opportunity to explore and manipulate representations (Eisenhart et al., 1993; Moreno & Mayer, 1999; Moyer, Niezgoda, & Stanley, 2005). Even the learning of basic facts is facilitated by a good understanding of number concepts (Crespo, Kyriakides, & McGee, 2005; Jordan, 2010; Jordan, Glutting, & Ramineni, 2010; Jordan, Hanich, & Kaplan, 2003). Without a solid understanding of mathematical concepts, mathematics becomes a series of rote procedures (Ginsberg, 1997; Poncy, Duhon, Lee, & Key, 2010; Rittle-Johnson, Siegler, & Alibali, 2001; Wood & Sellers, 1997).

Barriers to Conceptual Understanding (Comprehension of Mathematical Concepts, Operations, and Relations)

Number Sense

Understanding math concepts can be difficult for many students. At the heart of this understanding is something called "number sense"—the sense of what numbers mean and a flexibility in using numbers in mental math, making estimations and comparisons, and using math in everyday activities. Students with good number sense are able to recognize patterns in numbers, represent numbers in different ways, and use different procedures for computation (including ones that they invent themselves). Students with good number sense can use their estimation skills to tell whether a computation is incorrect. For example, when such students are adding the fractions 7/8 and 8/9, estimating tells them that the answer should be a little less than 2. The recognition of such gross errors becomes automatic, rather than part of an additional checking procedure.

Many students struggle with math because they have poor number sense. For them, math is an arbitrary, rote system to be memorized. For example, although they may be able to recite the multiplication tables, they do not understand the concept of multiplication and wouldn't think of using repeated addition as a different way to solve multiplication problems. Similarly, although they may understand fractions as a part of a whole—for example,

—they may not think of fractions in other ways, such as a subset of a group of objects,

or as a ratio or proportion, as in

For each child there are 2 cookies. 1 child/2 cookies

$$\frac{1 \text{ child}}{2 \text{ cookies}}$$

Understanding and relating different representations of math concepts are also critical to conceptual understanding. Students, for example, need to see the following representations as showing the same concept (adding 2 and 3):

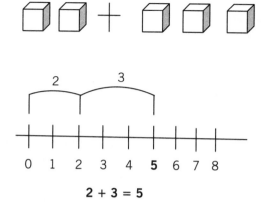

$$2 + 3 = 5$$

Connecting Prior Knowledge

Another important factor in understanding mathematical concepts is the ability to connect what is being learned to prior knowledge. Many educators consider math a unique subject, in that learners need to understand a variety of interdependent concepts and skills that are applied across many different areas of math (e.g., algebra, geometry, probability). Also, learning new concepts depends on mastery of earlier ones. When students don't make the connections between what they are currently studying and what they have already learned, math becomes a series of unrelated topics that require massive amounts of rote memorization with little understanding.

The problem is compounded by current math curricula, which have been described as "a mile wide and an inch deep" (Cogan & Schmidt, 1999, p. 2). There is a push to cover many topics in any given year, but little time is allowed for students to develop a deep understanding that they can sustain. Furthermore, while most students enter school with a basic awareness of numbers, they quickly abandon this intuitive understanding when confronted with formal math education. They begin to focus on learning the "one right way" to solve a problem and believe that there is always only one correct solution. This focus pushes the goal of mathematics away from understanding and toward learning a massive number of procedures, which students may apply incorrectly in a variety of scenarios.

Interpretation of Language and Symbols

Also contributing to the understanding of mathematical concepts is interpreting the language and symbols of math. Words such as "average" can have one meaning in everyday language and a different, more precise definition in mathematics. Similarly, students must learn to interpret mathematical notations as simple as

$$5 < 8$$

to ones as complex as

$$x = \frac{-b \pm \sqrt{b^2 - 4ac}}{2a}$$

Interpreting these math "sentences" can be a challenge for many students. An example of the difficulty imposed by the symbol system can be seen in how students interpret the equals sign (=). Students often misinterpret this sign to mean that the problem is to the left of the equals sign and the solution to the right, as in the problem below:

$$7 + 2 = \underline{\quad}$$

The solution to this problem is 9, which most elementary and middle school students solve correctly. However, when they are presented with a problem such as

$$7 + 2 = \underline{\quad} + 4$$

a frequent answer is 9. Many students do not interpret the equals sign as meaning that the values on each side must be the same.

Students are frequently asked to demonstrate their conceptual understanding of math by solving word problems. Yet this format imposes barriers for many students, and not just those who have difficulty with reading. Students who are successful with these problems are able to create a mental model of each problem situation and use this model to find a solution. However, many students instead look for key words that suggest a solution. The problem with this approach can be seen in the following:

Matt has 5 apples. He has 3 more than Sally.

How many apples does Sally have?

A student who uses a key word approach will interpret the word "more" to mean "add" and give 8 as the solution to the problem. The difficulty is compounded by the fact that some math textbooks do not present a variety of formats for word problems, which can inadvertently encourage students to use the key word approach. Yet this approach is not only frequently ineffective, but also has been shown to interfere with conceptual understanding as well as strategy development. A further barrier with problems such as this is the deceptively simple yet confusing language structure that is often found in word problems, particularly in the early grades.

MATH AND STRATEGIC NETWORKS

Once students have a fundamental understanding of math concepts, they must still learn the skills to manipulate those concepts. Strategic networks include both networks that control routine actions or procedures and those we use to generate active strategies for solving problems. Strategic actions are heavily dependent on the goal and the context in which the actions will occur (Campanella & Shallice, 2011; Cooper, Shallice, & Faringdon, 1995; Dehaene, 1997; Jeannerod, 1997). In order for a student to be an effective learner and problem solver, it is essential that basic skills and procedures become routine or automatic, allowing the student to put more attention and effort into applying conceptual knowledge (Gersten & Chard, 1999; Hiebert & Lefevre, 1986; Jordan et al., 2003, 2010). However, the student also must be able to select and order the appropriate procedures and to monitor their effectiveness in attaining a goal or solving a problem (Cary & Carlson, 1999; Hiebert & Lefevre, 1986; Lesh & Harel, 2003; Pressley, 1991). Students also need to know how to select appropriate strategies and to organize information effectively in order to solve complex problems (Jitendra, DiPipi, & Perron-Jones, 2002; Siegler, 2003).

Barriers to Procedural Fluency

Learning and Recalling Facts and Algorithms

A major barrier to procedural fluency is the difficulty some students have with learning and recalling basic facts and algorithms. Most students follow a predictable pattern when learning basic facts. For example, when calculating "2 + 3," they begin by holding up two fingers on one hand and three on the other, then counting all the fingers (counting all). The next step is called "counting on." Now students realize that they can start with two (the number of fingers on the first hand) and count up—3, 4, 5—to get to the total. Next they learn that the order doesn't matter; they can start with the larger number (3) and count up (4, 5). Going through this process supports students in internalizing these basic facts.

In addition, students learn "doubles" (1 + 1 = 2; 2 + 2 = 4; etc.). They then use these doubles to help them recall other facts (e.g., 3 + 4 is the same as 3 + 3 and 1 more). Most children appear to go through these steps intuitively, and they find answers by using different steps as they are consolidating them into memory. In contrast, some never really get beyond the counting stage. For them, the lack of automaticity is a major hindrance to any higher-level problem solving. It's interesting that in general, these children do not have a problem with number sense—they can find the correct answer eventually—but their conscious effort is devoted to a skill that should be automatic. On the other hand, a procedure itself can be a barrier when students do not understand the math concept that underlies it. For example, some students who learn the procedure of cross-multiplying to reduce fractions may not actually understand why this works, and may apply it even when there is a simpler way to solve a problem.

Fluency with Tools

Procedural fluency also includes facility with the tools of mathematics, such as rulers, protractors, and calculators, as well as the ability to create legible and accurate written work. Consider the sample below from Brian, a 7-year-old second grader. His numbers are immature but legible, but when asked to write "seven plus two equals nine," he has confused the two methods of writing (horizontal and vertical) and ended up with a combination of both.

$$6 \quad \quad 2 \quad 3 \quad 4 \quad 7 \quad 4 \quad 62$$
$$3 \quad 2 \quad 8 \quad 9$$

$$7 + 2 =$$
$$\overline{9}$$
$$\begin{array}{r} 1\,7. \\ +2\,3 \\ \hline \end{array}$$
$$\begin{array}{r} 1\,9 \\ +\,3 \\ \hline \end{array}$$

$$9 - 6 =$$

$$\begin{array}{cc} 2 \setminus 1 & \frac{1}{2} \\ 2 \cdot 3 & \frac{2}{3} \end{array}$$

Although the computer is an invaluable asset for students with fine motor problems, for whom writing is difficult, it is currently not ideal for recording mathematical notation (e.g., writing Brian's problems above vertically), and some tools may be as hard to manipulate onscreen with a mouse as the physical tool may be.

Barriers to Strategic Competence (Ability to Formulate, Represent, and Solve Mathematical Problems)

Strategic competence draws on all aspects of executive function, which include setting goals, developing plans of action, managing information, and monitoring progress toward the goals. Solving mathematical problems does not mean completing simple calculations, but the approaches taken to solve more complex and difficult problems. Such an approach requires developing a plan or strategy for solving a problem, monitoring the plan, and making modifications to it along the way as needed. Being able to monitor one's own thinking during problem solving, and to ensure that the steps taken and solutions obtained make sense in the context of the question asked, is critical to strategic competence.

Strategy Use

Students who struggle in math have been found to use fewer problem-solving strategies, and to use those they do have in an inflexible manner; when a strategy works for one problem, they expect it to work for all. Although general heuristics, such as "read, plan, solve, and check," may be useful to typically achieving students, they do not provide enough specific guidance for some students and may lead to even less flexibility. When students are first learning how to approach a problem, they tend to focus on the surface features, which can lead to inappropriate solution strategies. Some math textbooks reinforce this by presenting similarly structured word problems that do not foster a deeper understanding of appropriate strategies to use.

As mentioned above, many students are poor at reading a problem and formulating a strategy for solving it; they focus instead on more superficial aspects, such as key words and numbers. Another problem arises when students attempt to create their own visual representation to help them understand how to solve a problem. Students who use this approach successfully are able to create schematic diagrams that represent the essence of the problem and to ignore irrelevant details. Those who are not successful tend to make drawings that include information that is not needed to solve the problem. For example, consider the following:

> Mary rode her bike 3 miles to Marla's house.
> Mary and Marla then took the bus and rode 4 miles.
> They got off and walked 1 mile to the ice cream store.
> How many miles did Mary travel?

A successful schematic diagram of the problem above would be something like this:

It contains the important information needed to solve the problem, with no irrelevant details. An unsuccessful drawing would be more like this:

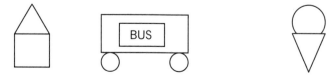

It contains elements of the story, but not the information needed to solve the problem. Students who use this approach rarely find the correct answer (van Garderen & Montague, 2003).

Working Memory

Another factor associated with skill in problem solving is "working memory," which is the ability to hold and manipulate information in one's mind. This mental "workspace" is critical for many cognitive activities, but particularly for those requiring the concurrent storage and processing of information, such as mental arithmetic. Working memory is important in problems that involve several steps and is needed to keep the question in mind when a student is solving any problem. In order to be successful problem solvers, students need to develop strategies for managing working memory (e.g., writing down the middle steps) and understand when to apply those strategies. All too often, students attempt to do problems "in their heads" in situations where the human brain is simply incapable of such tasks. Working memory is a strong predictor of students' problem-solving ability.

Barriers in Adaptive Reasoning (Capacity for Logical Thought, Reflection, Explanation, and Justification)

The ability to reason is essential to understanding mathematics. This ability includes developing and exploring ideas, making predictions and generalizations, and reaching and justifying conclusions. Applying mathematical reasoning means "making sense" of mathematics, not just following procedures or recalling facts.

MATH AND AFFECTIVE NETWORKS

The affective networks are essential structures in determining what is significant or important to an individual. These structures are critical in determining whether an object or situation is something to fear, something to crave, something to investigate, or something to ignore. The typical functioning of these structures thus results in the "why" of behavior—why we do what we do, or what we call "motivation" (Damasio, 1994; LeDoux, 1996).

What do these affective networks have to do with learning mathematics? They are not central either in recognizing the patterns of math or in performing its operations. They are central, however, in whether one engages in mathematics at all (Hoffman, 2010). At any given moment, there are many stimuli competing for attention and many possible actions to take. Whether a child will pay attention to the symbols of mathematics, or to the kinds of problem solving that mathematics entails, will depend in large part on the relative value (or importance) placed on those stimuli by the affective networks.

Barriers to Productive Disposition

Mathematics presents a wide variety of situations that may create anxiety and avoidance in students. Remembering the steps of an algorithm may prove stressful for a student with memory problems. The emphasis on communication of mathematical ideas creates a difficult situation for students with language disabilities and for those who are anxious about speaking in front of their peers. Good problem solvers need to feel comfortable trying out different approaches to a problem, and to know that there may not be only "one right way."

Many students develop the idea that they are "just not good at math." Students who view math as a threat frequently feel that they are unable to learn math and that "working harder" won't help. These students will trade accuracy for speed and tend to make more errors with complex problems. In fact, students in the United States are more likely to assume that innate ability is much more important than effort, and that it is socially acceptable (and often even desirable) not to put forth effort in learning mathematics.

Some students may find math boring. Textbooks that include pages of problems designed to practice a skill, for example, do not present a challenge for students who have already mastered that skill. Good teaching is largely the art of engagement—of finding what will motivate a child to learn mathematics and to feel confident in his or her ability in math.

Students' perceptions of the value of math drop from the middle grades on, as do their feelings of self-efficacy in math. It is tempting for teachers to avoid presenting mathematics in a real-life context, in favor of teaching the vast array of skills found in textbooks and curricula. Leaving such examples out, however, strengthens students' beliefs in the uselessness of math and deemphasizes conceptual understanding in favor of the wide but shallow curricula described by Cogan and Schmidt (1999).

HOW UDL CAN HELP

The barriers described above have an important impact on many students. Approximately 7% of students have a mathematics learning disability that interferes with their ability to learn concepts and/or procedures in one or more aspects of mathematics. An additional 35% can be described as students with mathematical difficulties; these are students who struggle to learn math for many of the reasons described above. In addition, students with motor or sensory impairments may have unique needs for accessing math content and demonstrating what they are learning. The UDL principles offer many options for all of these students (Mazzocco, 2007). Below are both low-tech and high-tech examples of ways in which the UDL principles can support students who are struggling with mathematics.

Supporting Recognition Networks

Customize How Information Is Presented

Students may seem to have difficulty with math because of the way the content is presented. Math text pages often contain myriad text descriptions, illustrations, instructions, examples, and problems to solve, all of which can leave a student unsure of how to proceed. Simplifying the page layout and presenting less information on a page can help students to focus on the math. Other strategies that can help are using larger fonts, presenting fewer problems on a page, and providing lines or answer boxes for students to use. Creating worksheets in Microsoft Word or another word-processing program is a way to make pages that can be customized in these ways. Special consideration is needed for students with sensory deficits, such as blindness. Often the traditional formats are not appropriate for these students because they are inaccessible to them. In such cases, alternative formats are needed to represent concepts. A good resource for these students is the website of the Texas School for the Blind and Visually Impaired (*http://www.tsbvi.edu/math*).

Define Vocabulary and Symbols; Decode Mathematical Notation

Math has specific language and symbols that students need to learn. Often words that are commonly used, such as "difference," have specific meanings in math, and students need to know how to use them correctly. Other words, such as "polynomial," are a part of a specialized math vocabulary. In addition, math has its own set of symbols, and students need to understand their meanings. Students may need additional supports, such as math dictionaries and previews of new vocabulary, to help them understand the language of mathematics. Several multimedia math dictionaries are available online. The Harcourt Math Glossary (*http://www.harcourtschool.com/glossary/math2/index_temp.html*) is designed for students from kindergarten through sixth grade and includes both audio and visual images. The Interactive Mathematics Dictionary (*http://intermath.coe.uga.edu/dictnary/homepg.asp*) is designed for all grades and includes animations and interactive features as a part of its definitions.

Illustrate Key Concepts with Different Representations

Understanding mathematics requires recognizing and interpreting number concepts represented symbolically, linguistically, and in physical representations. For example, the concept that 5 is a larger number than 3 can be represented as follows:

"Five is greater than three" (linguistic)

5 > 3 (symbolic)

<u>1</u> <u>2</u> <u>3</u> <u>4</u> <u>5</u> (physical—number line)

In addition, within each of these formats, the concept can be represented in more than one way. The statement "Three is less than five" is another representation, as is "3 < 5." Physically, we could represent the relationship between 3 and 5 by using counting chips, Base 10 Blocks, Cuisenaire Rods, or myriad other materials, each of which has different properties. It is particularly important not only that students recognize mathematical concepts presented in each of these formats, but that they recognize the relationship between them.

Although we often think that presenting a concept through a variety of media and formats is best, this is not always the case. If the same concept is presented in different formats, it is important to choose the formats carefully to enhance that concept, so that students will not view each as representing a different idea. When the formats are chosen carefully, using multiple media and formats can enhance learning. When a new or unfamiliar format is used, however, it is important to be sure that students grasp the underlying meaning and are able to connect this new representation to ones that they already know. What often seems transparent to us as adults is not at all clear to our students.

Several websites offer math applets that are designed to support math concepts through different representations. The National Library of Virtual Manipulatives (*http://nlvm.usu.edu*) is a library of web-based interactive virtual manipulatives for elementary and middle school students. Interactivate (*http://www.shodor.org/interactivate*), from the Shodor Educational Foundation, includes over 150 tools and activities. Illuminations (*http://illuminations.nctm.org*), developed through a partnership between the NCTM and MarcoPolo, includes interactive tools that support exploration of math concepts categorized by grade level and linked to the NCTM Standards. A free, dynamic program designed for middle and high school students is GeoGebra (*http://www.geogebra.org/cms*), which connects algebra, geometry, statistics, and calculus, with interactive graphs and tables.

Provide or Activate Background Knowledge; Connect New Knowledge to Previously Learned

New knowledge is best learned when it is incorporated into what has been previously learned. One of the NCTM Standards explicitly states the importance of connecting new learning to what has been previously learned (NCTM, 2000). Students need to understand applications of mathematical concepts to everyday life. They also need to understand the math they are learning within an overall framework of mathematical concepts. We want to create increasingly complex representations of mathematical content areas—a mathematical "web."

Highlight Critical Features, Big Ideas, and Relationships

Students learn mathematical structure and rules by recognizing critical elements and then generating and testing hypotheses about these elements. We must carefully select examples of the concepts we are teaching, and make sure that students focus on the relevant features. Novice learners tend to focus on superficial elements rather than the underlying structure. So when introducing new information, we should explicitly highlight the significant structural features, and when we use a variety of formats, we need to be sure that the students see the structural similarities. "Highlighting" also can be done by creating a worksheet for students to use with manipulatives that help them focus on their meaning. Examples should be carefully selected, based in students' current understanding of the concept, and used to extend it. If an example presents something from a new perspective, it should be clearly linked to one that the learners already understand. Several of the math applet sites mentioned above include activities that teachers can use to help students focus on the important features.

Support Transfer

Often students learn math concepts in an isolated fashion; although they may be able to use these concepts with familiar problems, they do not see how to transfer their application to new situations. Students demonstrate a true understanding of math concepts only when they can apply them in a variety of situations. It is important to provide them with these novel situations and guide them to understand they relate to the more familiar ones. Math WebQuests (*http://www.webquest. org*) are one way to provide novel situations for learning and practicing math concepts.

Supporting Strategic Networks

Provide Varied Ways to Interact and Respond

Students can demonstrate what they have learned in many ways other than traditional pencil-and-paper testing. Open-ended assignments, such as creating a game and determining its rules, allow students to apply knowledge in a new way. Students may participate in projects or create simulations as a group, with each student taking responsibility for a part.

It is important that the method chosen for demonstrating knowledge does not pose its own problems. For example, a student who has trouble with handwriting may be more successful when explaining answers orally rather than in writing. Similarly, a student who becomes anxious when talking in class can write his or her explanations. The source of math difficulties may not be the math itself, but in the ability to express the answers. Encouraging students to respond in other ways will help identify where any misunderstanding is coming from. Special consideration must be taken for a student with a physical disability that interferes with writing or speaking. For students who have difficulty with writing and drawing, the FX MathPack from Efofex (*http://www.efofex.com/mathpack.php*) includes tools that allow teachers and students to create drawings, symbols, graphs, and equations in mathematics. A 30-day free trial is available, and Efofex provides its products free of charge to students with special needs. MathType (*http://www.dessci.com/en/products/ mathtype*), available from Design Science, can be used to create accessible math content that can be read with most screen readers and rendered in math Braille. It also works with Microsoft Word to support students who have difficulty with writing math equations.

Provide Scaffolds for Practice and Performance

Many processes that are part of mathematical thinking can be modeled for students. For example, a teacher may use a "think-aloud" to describe the reasoning process used in deciding what method of estimation would be best for a specific problem. Alternatively, this reasoning can be given to students in text and illustrations. For skills that should be routine or automatic, such as applying an algorithm, the steps can be posted in the room as a reference, or calculators can be made available. Students also may be given worked-out examples of problems that they can use as references.

Many skills in mathematics—such as recalling basic facts, the steps in algorithms, or rules for estimation; creating data displays; or using a calculator—need to be routine or automatic in order to be used effectively. If a student puts extra effort into any of these, then less effort is available for the higher-order thinking necessary for problem solving. Practicing, however, does not mean merely rote drill. Supported practice helps students place the skill in a context so that they can know when and how to draw on this skill, both in the problems presented in mathematics classes and in everyday life. Many math applets can provide students with supported practice. For a review, see Center for Implementing Technology in Education (2008).

Provide Appropriate Tools

Other considerations are the supports students may need when a skill is not automatic. For example, many students can apply their conceptual understanding of multiplication to solve relatively complex problems, even though they may not remember all the steps of the multiplication algorithm. If they are required to do the calculations, most of their energy will be devoted to remembering these steps, rather than to analyzing the problem and applying their conceptual knowledge. Providing support for the calculations, such as using a calculator or pairing with a student who is good at computation, will ensure that such students have ample opportunities to develop and refine their problem-solving skills. Microsoft Mathematics (*http://www.microsoft.com/education/en-us/teachers/guides/Pages/Mathematics-guide.aspx*) contains several tools for both teachers and students.

Support Planning and Strategy Development

Teachers need to present situations that require students to select, apply, and adapt strategies to solve a novel problem (one in which the solution is not obvious or for which there can be more than one answer). These types of problems encourage students to reflect on the problem-solving process they are using and whether or not it is effective. The situations provided should be ones in which more than one approach will work and ones in which the student must reflect on progress and make adjustments. The goal of these opportunities is not necessarily for students to be correct, but for them to learn to apply their skills effectively, to reflect on their process as they work, and to see alternative approaches that may also be appropriate. Cut the Knot (*http://www.cut-the-knot.org*) is a website that contains games, puzzles, paradoxes, illusions, and many other types of activities that can be used to promote problem solving and reflection. Cyberchase, from PBSKids (*http://pbskids. org/cyberchase*), is an adventure series and website designed to helps kids develop strong math and problem-solving skills.

Facilitate Managing Information and Resources

Often math problems are complex, requiring several steps and the need to draw on and keep track of information from several sources. Many students do not have good strategies for keeping information in an organized manner so that they can use it efficiently. They can benefit from supports such as graphic organizers to serve this purpose. Tables and graphs can also be useful in organizing information; students need to learn the benefits of different formats of these tools. Some students may even benefit from learning how to use scratch paper to work out problems and keep track of data. Explaining to students the idea of working memory, so that they understand why it is fundamentally necessary to use these types of notes to manage their information, may be helpful as well. Inspiration (*http://www.inspiration.com/Inspiration*) is a multimedia concept-mapping tool that many find valuable for organizing ideas and information. A version for young children, Kidspiration (*http://www.inspiration.com/Kidspiration*), is also available. Both programs have a 30-day free trial.

Enhance Capacity for Monitoring Progress

Understanding of number concepts and their applications is enhanced when students are helped to analyze errors and find ways to correct them. Students should be encouraged to question their own work and to find multiple solutions to problems. Monitoring progress, however, does not mean only evaluating completed work. It should be done throughout each problem to ensure correct reasoning behind the answer and to minimize the chance that the entire problem needs to be erased upon discovering a wrong answer at the end. Teachers also need to be aware of situations in which students need extra support during monitoring because of limitations in background knowledge or necessary procedures.

Supporting Affective Networks

Offer Choices

Providing students with choices of content and tools can increase their interest in and enthusiasm for learning particular concepts and skills. The opportunity to link current learning to areas of particular interest can make learning easier. Students also are more likely to practice skills when these are embedded in activities that they enjoy. Students can be given choices about the math itself as well. For example, when the textbook has several similar problems, students can select the three that they want to solve, rather than doing all.

Enhance Relevance, Value, and Authenticity; Reduce Threats, Distractions

Many students enjoy the types of multimedia presentations offered by many software programs, but there are some who find this context overwhelming. Students need to have some control over the sights and sounds of their learning environment whenever possible.

Many students feel they cannot succeed at mathematics because they have trouble remembering the number facts and algorithms that are needed to find these types of answers. Other students enjoy the preciseness of facts and algorithms, but are uncomfortable in the more open-ended, problem-solving aspect of mathematics, where there may be more than one correct answer or several ways to find the answer. Both types of students need to be supported in the classroom.

Ideally, the rewards of learning mathematics should be intrinsic to the subject. However, in many situations, we need to provide external rewards. Embedding the learning in a game or puzzle format is one way to do this. Teachers also can offer prizes as rewards for student work, but should keep in mind that the ultimate goal should be to move toward intrinsic rewards whenever possible.

Vary Levels of Challenge and Support

Students need tasks that are challenging—not so easy that they become boring, or so difficult that they are viewed as requiring too much effort. This optimal level of challenge varies from student to student; it also varies for individual students, depending on the task, the context, and other factors not directly related to learning (such as concerns at home). Some students may feel comfortable moving forward in small steps, with frequent opportunities to practice what they are learning. Others enjoy the challenge of a larger, open-ended learning situation. Adjustable levels of challenge will allow both of these groups of students to work at their optimal level of challenge without feeling threatened by failure.

Increase Mastery-Oriented Feedback

Feedback is essential to the development of reasoning and problem-solving strategies. Appropriate feedback can help students develop a sense that their efforts are paying off and that they can be successful in math. Using the language of mathematics in providing feedback will help students learn to use such communication as a strategy for reflection on their work. Feedback should also help students pinpoint problems in their thinking process and alternative approaches to try; help them make judgments about the reasonableness of their solutions; and encourage them to evaluate the mathematical thinking and strategies of others. Feedback is necessary as well when students are learning the skills that need to become routine or automatic. For the feedback to be relevant, it should not merely indicate whether or not a student has performed correctly, but should help the student see what to change in order to be correct. For example, many students make errors in subtraction because of problems in regrouping. Feedback for these students might include how regrouping is related to place value.

CONCLUSION

Math has become increasingly emphasized in the current educational climate. Teachers can no longer afford to say that "some students are just not good at math." By applying the principles of UDL to math instruction and assessment, teachers can create flexible learning environments that support conceptual understanding, procedural fluency, strategic competence, and adaptive reasoning, while at the same time showing students that math is useful and is a subject that they can master. UDL is a valuable way to help all students to become successful in learning math.

REFERENCES

Brown, S. A., & Mehilos, M. (2010). Using tables to bridge arithmetic and algebra. *Mathematics Teaching in the Middle School, 15*(9), 532–538.

Campanella, F., & Shallice, T. (2011). Manipulability and object recognition: Is manipulability a semantic feature? *Experimental Brain Research, 208*(3), 369–383.

Cary, M., & Carlson, R. A. (1999). External support and the development of problem-solving routines. *Journal of Experimental Psychology: Learning, Memory, and Cognition, 25*(4), 1053–1070.

Center for Implementing Technology in Education. (2008). Practicing math online: Fun, free, and cool! Retrieved from *http://www.ldonline.org/article/24850.*

Cogan, L. S., & Schmidt, W. H. (1999, Fall). Middle school math reform. *Middle Matters, 8,* 2–3.

Cooper, R., Shallice, T., & Faringdon, J. (1995). Symbolic and continuous processes in the automatic selection of actions. In J. Hallam (Ed.), *Hybrid problems, hybrid solutions* (pp. 27–37). Amsterdam: IOS Press.

Crespo, S. M., Kyriakides, A. O., & McGee, S. (2005). Nothing "basic" about basic facts: Exploring addition facts with fourth graders. *Teaching Children Mathematics, 12*(2), 60–67.

Damasio, A. R. (1994). *Descartes' error: Emotion, reason, and the human brain.* New York: Putnam.

Dehaene, S. (1997). *The number sense: How the mind creates mathematics.* New York: Oxford University Press.

Eisenhart, M., Borko, H., Underhill, R., Brown, C., Jones, D., & Agard, P. (1993). Conceptual recognition falls through the cracks: Complexities of learning to teach mathematics for understanding. *Journal for Research in Mathematics Education, 24*(1), 8–40.

Gersten, R., & Chard, D. (1999). Number sense: Rethinking arithmetic instruction for students with mathematical disabilities. *Journal of Special Education, 44,* 18–28.

Ginsberg, H. P. (1997). Mathematics learning disabilities: A view from developmental psychology. *Journal of Learning Disabilities, 30*(1), 20–33.

Hasselbring, T. S., & Moore, P. R. (1996). Developing mathematical literacy through the use of contextualized learning environments. *Journal of Computing in Childhood Education, 7*(3–4), 199–222.

Hiebert, J., & Lefevre, P. (1986). Conceptual and procedural recognition in mathematics: An introductory analysis. In J. Hiebert (Ed.), *Conceptual and procedural recognition: The case of mathematics* (pp. 1–27). Hillsdale, NJ: Erlbaum.

Hoffman, B. (2010). I think I can, but I'm afraid to try: The role of self-efficacy beliefs and mathematics anxiety in mathematics problem-solving efficiency. *Learning and Individual Differences, 20*(3), 276–283.

Jeannerod, M. (1997). *The cognitive neuroscience of action.* Cambridge, MA: Blackwell.

Jitendra, A., DiPipi, C. M., & Perron-Jones, N. (2002). An exploratory study of schema-based word-problem-solving instruction for middle school students with learning disabilities: An emphasis on conceptual and procedural understanding. *Journal of Special Education, 36*(1), 23–38.

Jordan, N. C. (2010). Early predictors of mathematics achievement and mathematics learning difficulties. In R. E. Tremblay, R. G. Barr, R. D. Peters, & M. Boivin (Eds.), *Encyclopedia on early childhood development (online)* (pp. 1–6). Montréal: Centre of Excellence for Early Childhood Development. Retrieved February 23, 2012, from *http://www.child-encyclopedia.com/documents/JordanANGXP.pdf.*

Jordan, N. C., Glutting, J., & Ramineni, C. (2010). The importance of number sense to mathematics achievement in first and third grades. *Learning and Individual Differences, 20,* 82–88.

Jordan, N. C., Hanich, L. B., & Kaplan, D. (2003). Arithmetic fact mastery in young children: A longitudinal investigation. *Journal of Experimental Child Psychology, 85,* 103–119.

LeDoux, J. (1996). *The emotional brain.* New York: Simon & Schuster.

Lesh, R., & Harel, G. (2003). Problem solving, modeling, and local conceptual development. *Mathematical Thinking and Learning, 5*(2–3), 157–189.

Marshall, A. M., Superfine, A. C., & Canty, R. S. (2010). Star students make connections:

Discover strategies to engage young math students in competently using multiple representations. *Teaching Children Mathematics, 17*(1), 38–47.

Mazzocco, M. M. M. (2007). Defining and differentiating mathematical learning disabilities and difficulties. In D. Berch & M. M. M. Mazzocco (Eds.), *Why is math so hard for some children?: The nature and origins of mathematical learning difficulties and disabilities* (pp. 29–48). Baltimore: Brookes.

Moreno, R., & Mayer, R. E. (1999). Multimedia-supported metaphors for meaning making in mathematics. *Cognition and Instruction, 17*(3), 215–248.

Moyer, P. S., Niezgoda, D., & Stanley, J. (2005). Young children's use of virtual manipulatives and other forms of mathematical representations. In W. J. Masalaski & P. C. Elliott (Eds.), *Technology-supported mathematics learning environments* (pp. 17–34). Reston, VA: National Council of Teachers of Mathematics.

National Council of Teachers of Mathematics (NCTM). (1998). An NCTM statement of beliefs. *NCTM News Bulletin, 35*(1), 5.

National Council of Teachers of Mathematics (NCTM). (2000). *Principles and standards for school mathematics.* Reston, VA: Author.

National Research Council. (2001). *Adding it up: Helping children learn mathematics.* Washington, DC: National Academies Press.

Poncy, B., Duhon, G., Lee, S., & Key, A. (2010). Evaluation of techniques to promote generalization with basic math fact skills. *Journal of Behavioral Education, 19*(1), 76–92.

Pressley, M. (1991). Can learning-disabled children become good information processors?: How can we find out? In V. Feagans, E. J. Short, & L. J. Meltzer (Eds.), *Subtypes of learning disabilities: Theoretical perspectives and research* (pp. 137–162). Hillsdale, NJ: Erlbaum.

Rittle-Johnson, B., Siegler, R. S., & Alibali, M. W. (2001). Developing conceptual understanding and procedural skill in mathematics: An iterative process. *Journal of Educational Psychology, 93*(2), 346–362.

Siegler, R. S. (2003). Implications of cognitive science research for mathematics education. In J. Kilpatrick, W. B. Martin, & D. E. Schifter (Eds.), *A research companion to principles and standards for school mathematics* (pp. 219–233). Reston, VA: National Council of Teachers of Mathematics.

Smith, L. B., & Katz, D. B. (1996). Activity-dependent processes in perceptual and cognitive development. In R. Gelman & T. Kit-Fong (Eds.), *Perceptual and cognitive development* (2nd ed., pp. 413–445). New York: Academic Press.

Thelen, E., & Smith, L. B. (1994). *A dynamic systems approach to the development of cognition and action.* Cambridge, MA: MIT Press.

van Garderen, D., & Montague, M. (2003). Visual–spatial representation, mathematical problem solving and students of varying abilities. *Learning Disabilities Research and Practice, 18*(4), 246–254.

Wood, T., & Sellers, P. (1997). Deepening the analysis: Longitudinal assessment of a problem-centered mathematics program. *Journal of Research in Mathematics Education, 28*(2), 163–186.

CHAPTER 7

Doing History the Universal Design for Learning Way

KRISTIN H. ROBINSON and ANNE MEYER

Most of us learned history in classrooms where teacher talk and textbooks were the sources of information. Our textbooks and teachers probably presented history as a neatly packaged set of facts to memorize—one "true" story whose narrative was defined by a small group of scholars in the field. But a different approach, often called "Doing History," is emerging. Doing History encourages students to think and work the way historians do (Seixas, 1993; Wineburg, 2001).

Specifically, this problem-based inquiry approach teaches students to apply history-related strategies to multiple and often contradictory sources—such as letters, newspaper articles, images, artworks, or individual accounts—to glean insight into historical events and trends. These strategies include qualifying, corroborating, contextualizing, and synthesizing primary sources in order for students to develop their own understanding of what happened. In doing so, they learn the very kinds of critical reasoning they need to participate as global citizens in our complex, information-saturated world.

Doing History can be engaging and effective, but can also be challenging for both students and teachers (De La Paz, 2005; Van Sledright, 2002), in part because the traditional "teacher talk, textbooks" model remains dominant in teacher preparation and in schools. The diversity of learners in a given classroom—with differences in preparedness, language, cultural background, ability, and interests—also present a challenge. Doing History requires not only close teacher involvement (Saye & Brush, 2006), but also support for diverse learners (De La Paz, 2005).

However, these apparent challenges actually create a unique opportunity for educators and publishers to transform history and social studies instruction in important ways. The key is Universal Design for Learning (UDL). Using the UDL Guidelines (see Lapinski, Gravel, & Rose, Chapter 2, this volume), we can rethink curricular goals, methods, materials, and assessments. We can also apply digital technology in the service of the newly conceptualized curriculum. By reshaping the curriculum itself, we create new teaching and learning opportunities for all involved.

In this chapter, we describe some of the insights we gained during a multiyear project aimed at developing a digital learning environment, designed according to UDL principles, to support a Doing History approach. This work, done in collaboration with Grant R. Miller, showed us that the UDL approach to Doing History proves to be a powerful way to help students develop the mindsets of professional historians, together with the skills to question and challenge primary sources, develop rich content knowledge, and become engaged investigators of the past.

ADDRESSING CHALLENGES POSED
BY THE TRADITIONAL CURRICULUM

Traditional curriculum materials are too inflexible to provide all learners with genuine opportunities for Doing History. The 2006 National Assessment of Educational Progress (NAEP) showed that only 13% of high school seniors performed at a "proficient" level in U.S. history, and that fewer than half (47%) achieved a "basic" score (National Center for Education Statistics, 2007). The results were only slightly better than those of earlier assessments in 2001 and 1994. In analyzing the disappointing 2001 results, the National Center for Education Statistics (2002) found one promising connection: High student scores on the NAEP history test were correlated with their teachers' use of primary sources in the classroom. However, the deep content knowledge that teachers need in order to use flexible, primary source materials is rare.

The predominant textbook-oriented approach to teaching social studies and history presents learning barriers for all. Students and teachers alike are justifiably "turned off" by rote memorization of events and places that neither are connected to their lives nor support the development of applicable understandings and skills. The flat and fixed nature of print is antithetical to the active, engaged exploration on which the discipline of history is built.

The barriers inherent in the traditional, print-based curriculum go beyond mere disengagement. Many social studies and history textbook authors may inappropriately assume that all students share the same background knowledge, and therefore may provide incomplete or inadequate explanations of events. Nor do many textbooks explain learning goals clearly to students, leaving them unclear about why they are studying a particular person, event, or period (Beck, McKeown, & Gromoll, 1989).

The impact of these limitations is felt even more strongly in a diverse class-room, where learners with different backgrounds, home languages, and abilities are supposed to be guaranteed equal opportunities to learn. Even when textbooks do include prompting questions, annotated images, and connections to current events and issues, the limitations of the print medium are inescapable. Print is a fixed medium that cannot be adjusted or acted upon in a meaningful way; thus, by its very nature, it is not flexible and responsive to individual differences.

The Doing History approach, when taught using digital materials designed according to UDL principles, overcomes some of the more obvious barriers to learn-ing posed by the textbook-based model. Why is this so? The Doing History inquiry-based instructional model encourages diverse, flexible approaches to acquiring information, performing learning tasks, and staying motivated and engaged in learning. Research shows that primary sources materials provide students with multiple perspectives on historical events and encourage them to actively construct historical understanding (Spoehr & Spoehr, 1994; Wineburg, 1991). Working with primary sources allows students to form "a richer and more detailed mental model of that event, thus enhancing content knowledge" more than passively receiving information can (Stahl, Hynd, Britton, McNish, & Bousquet, 1996, p. 434).

Still, this approach does pose new challenges for students and teachers (De La Paz, 2005; VanSledright, 2002). Research has shown that students who were assigned a specific task and exposed to multiple source documents did not gain more com-plex understandings or enhance their historical inquiry skills. Exposure to mul-tiple sources is necessary but not sufficient for developing these skills. Students also require explicit instruction and support in how to contextualize information; how to find, analyze, and interpret documents in order to make meaning; and how to express their findings persuasively—in short, how to think and act like historians (Stahl et al., 1996).

Primary sources also present their own barriers. For example, obsolete vocabu-lary and syntax can be unintelligible for today's learners. Many documents selected for this kind of instruction are also text-heavy, posing barriers to students who have difficulty with decoding or who lack background knowledge. Also, students new to the approach and students with learning challenges often find it difficult to deter-mine what part of an early document is most relevant to their question, or to decide which documents are more reliable than others.

Researchers have found that both teachers and students learn history content more effectively if they engage in higher-order, discipline-specific thinking, and use primary sources as a historian would (Levstik & Barton, 2011; Gabella, 1994). Researchers have also shown that teachers can support and engage diverse learners through flexible digital curricula—instructional tools and methods found in the framework of UDL (Rose & Meyer, 2002). Combining these two frameworks pro-vides a powerful new approach to teaching history.

DOING HISTORY THE UDL WAY

Combining the engaging, active Doing History approach with UDL draws on the power and flexibility of digital multimedia to maximize opportunities for diverse learners to participate actively in historical inquiry. First, digital versions of primary sources in multiple media are widely available from libraries, museums, and universities,[1] and can be enhanced in various ways to make them more widely accessible. Second, offering varied digital tools for expression gives students the opportunity to express their knowledge in ways that enable them to best demonstrate what they know. Third, Doing History within a digital environment can offer students options for engaging with and building enthusiasm for historical inquiry itself. In our discussion of materials below, we offer one example of a UDL digital learning environment developed with CAST's UDL Book Builder, a free online tool (*http://bookbuilder.cast.org*). We use this example only to illustrate ideas; with myriad web-based tools available free or at low cost, there are many avenues for creating such environments.

The framework of UDL is designed to help students become expert learners—learners who have gained knowledge, skills, and the desire to learn more. One key objective is providing the right balance of challenge and support in any learning experience, so that both teachers and learners can focus on what really matters—reaching the goals of the lesson itself. Too much challenge frustrates learners; not enough challenge fails to engage them. Another key objective is providing all students with learning pathways that are consistent with and supportive of their interests, skills, abilities, and backgrounds. This balance is achieved by offering options for how students may do the following (Rose & Meyer, 2002):

- Acquire information (the "what" of learning).
- Approach learning tasks and express themselves (the "how" of learning).
- Stay motivated and engaged (the "why" of learning).

In the remainder of the chapter, we explain how these core principles guide the design and implementation of Doing History the UDL way. This approach combines the power of authentic primary sources in multiple media, discipline-specific historical inquiry strategies, and options for engaging diverse learners in active exploration of historical questions. We consider the four key elements of curriculum—instructional goals, materials, methods, and assessments—as reframed through Doing History and UDL. Goals and materials are discussed first; methods and assessments are discussed in a later section.

---

[1]For example, see the Library of Congress's American Memory (*http://memory.loc.gov*), Primary Sources at Yale University (*http://www.yale.edu/collections_collaborative/primarysources*), and the National Archives (*http://www.archives.gov*).

Instructional Goals

Clear goals for learning guide every curriculum consideration. To engage students and enable them to evaluate their own progress, we need to express learning goals, offer optional paths for achieving the goals, convey criteria for success, and build explicit ties to students' lives. Fuzzy goals confuse teachers and learners alike—and risk unnecessary failure.

Often goals or standards for learning are worded so that the goals and the means for reaching them are inextricably linked in a way that creates barriers to success for some learners. For example, consider these directions: "Read the section about the Boston Massacre in the text. Write an essay explaining the forces that contributed to this event." The actual learning goal, stated from a UDL perspective, is this: "Using historical inquiry strategies, students will develop and be able to express, citing evidence, their viewpoint on what forces contributed to the Boston Massacre." But the goal as expressed in these directions offers only one avenue for accessing the content (reading text) and only one means of expressing knowledge (writing an essay). Students who struggle with decoding words or writing may be perfectly capable of understanding the content and expressing their knowledge through other avenues. The way this assignment is constructed impedes their ability to function at their highest cognitive level and participate fully in the assignment.

Setting the goals within a UDL framework may look as follows:

"During this lesson, you will think about what it means to be someone involved in a deadly shooting—the Boston Massacre. As you go through this unit, you will:

- Gain an understanding of the process of historical inquiry by reading and working through the model.
- Use the process of historical inquiry to conduct your own research.
- Present your argument about your topic through an essay, PowerPoint, video, poster, or other approved format. If you would like to present in another format, please discuss with me."

When the directions start with a clear goal, separated from the means of achieving it, the assignment can be written or otherwise completed in an inclusive manner—leaving open to students various options for obtaining the knowledge, applying strategies, and expressing what they know.

Of course, there may be many cases where reading text and producing a written essay actually are the learning goals. In such cases, the assignment must require both reading and writing. However, a UDL approach would include a variety of pathways to reach this result as well. The goal is comprehension of the text, not learning to decode words. In this case, it would be appropriate to supply text-to-speech (TTS) support for reading text. Similarly, the point of the essay is clear expression of ideas. Tools to support mechanics (such as spell check), and multimedia tools (such as drawing or audio recording) that help students organize their thinking, can help them reach the goal in the way that works best for them.

Within the UDL framework, goals are disaggregated from the means to achieve them, and multiple pathways to success are offered. UDL goals provide students with clear learning goals, clear criteria for success, and flexible pathways to achieving success.

Materials

What do materials look like when students are Doing History the UDL way? Whereas traditional social studies and history instruction relies primarily on textbooks, UDL calls for whatever materials are found to be appropriate and effective for helping learners meet the lesson goal. These may be text, but may also include images, audio, film, architecture, websites, and art. Some students understand best when reading text; others find graphic representations clearer. Still others understand information best when it is presented orally, and many find that combining text, images, or graphics with audio helps them put the pieces of a historical puzzle together. Opportunities to work toward the lesson goal should not be hamstrung by limited learning materials.

Doing History also suggests providing access to many types and sources of information and many pathways to success, all of which support student engagement. Providing an extensive set of sources in varied media from which students can select gives them options to choose the documents and media most meaningful and motivating for them.

Although it may seem daunting to assemble a wide variety of sources and media types, we have already seen glimpses of the huge array readily available from reliable web-based repositories. The digital environment extends the walls of the classroom and offers instant access to text, image, video, and audio sources in museum collections, national and local archives, historical societies, and so on. All these materials are immediately available to use as social studies and history resources in the classroom.

Yet the instant availability of a variety of sources does not ensure that all learners will easily be able to access and use them. Nor does collecting sources alone support students in learning the key discipline-specific strategies in historical inquiry, or in learning to build arguments with skillful use of citations. To maximize the power of the digital environment, a curriculum must be constructed with flexible embedded supports and challenges, as well as with options that can be accessed by different learners as appropriate for them. The UDL Guidelines (see Lapinski et al., Chapter 2) provide a framework for considering all the different ways to improve access to knowledge, development of strategic skill, and options for engagement to reach diverse learners and keep the learning goal front and center.

Support for a UDL approach to Doing History can be created by using readily available online tools and applications. For our example in this chapter, we have used a free online tool, CAST's UDL Book Builder (*http://bookbuilder.cast.org*). This tool is designed to support UDL authoring, and so it has some built-in features that take advantage of the power of digital media. Rather than "receiving" content in a passive way, students develop the skills they need to become expert learners of history. These skills will be the vehicle for greater depth in understanding historical content that was superficially understood in traditional instruction. Our example is just a single illustration of how to support students in accessing content, learning and applying discipline-specific strategies in history, and finding the right level of challenge and support to keep them engaged.

MAKING HISTORY: A UDL-BASED ONLINE ENVIRONMENT

Making History (Robinson, 2010) is a multimedia unit designed to model and support the development of historical inquiry skills. The lesson starts by providing the schema for students: an overview of learning support features, including TTS support, glossary links, and hyperlinks; and then an overview of the process of historical inquiry in the form of an outline, or "road map," for students. Students can listen to the page text by using the built-in TTS capability, and can access context-specific word meanings through embedded hyperlinks.[2]

The *Making History* ebook models historical inquiry by providing extended think-alouds of each stage of the process: building background information; creating essential questions; gathering sources; working with sources by collecting information, evaluating it, and applying it to each essential question; corroborating evidence; and synthesizing the information into an argument. Students are prompted at each stage of the process to apply the modeled skills to their own historical inquiry project.

Three online coaches support students in the recognition, action/expression, and engagement aspects of learning (corresponding to the three UDL principles) throughout the unit. Coach support is presented in two modes, text and audio, and students can reread or listen to coach support as needed. (See Figure 7.1 for examples of coaches.) Vocabulary is supported throughout the book via a multimedia glossary (Figure 7.2). Words and phrases are defined in student-friendly terms, and many definitions include images and audio to further support learners.

During each lesson, students can investigate several primary documents, including visual as well as text sources. Hyperlinks to the sources enable learners to study documents themselves and to engage in the process of making meaning with historical materials. Student response areas on the bottom of each page invite students to keep notes, respond to questions, and keep track of their work. Their responses can be collected into a single document and saved, along with prompts, questions, and page numbers for notes.

---

[2]To view the teacher and student versions of *Making History*, see the URLs provided in the Robinson (2010) entry in the References list.

FIGURE 7.1. Three coaches support students in the recognition, strategic, and affective aspects of learning (corresponding to the three UDL principles). From Robinson (2010). Copyright 2010 by CAST, Inc. All rights reserved. Used with permission.

This supported historical inquiry environment, *Making History,* is one approach to reducing the barriers presented by textbooks or inquiry-based instruction in a print-based context. This instructional environment models multiple document choices and supports the process of working with sources in different modalities. Historical inquiry, as an approach, promotes flexibility on what to do (choosing an area of study, forming an essential question, deciding what to learn) and why to do it as students create the purpose of their own inquiry.

The UDL digital environment at a basic level can remove unnecessary barriers to learning. For instance, if students cannot understand a text, they cannot understand what is being communicated. This is a significant barrier to what instructors want students to master: using inquiry skills to analyze and make meaning from multiple sources. Flexible digital documents provide access for all students, and a digital glossary provides just-in-time support for understanding words and phrases in

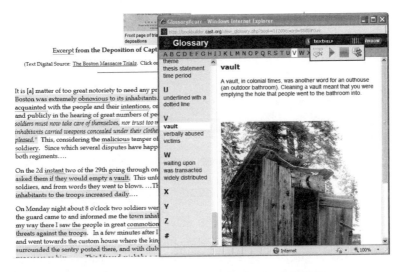

FIGURE 7.2. Vocabulary is supported through a multimedia glossary. From Robinson (2010). Copyright 2010 by CAST, Inc. All rights reserved. Used with permission.

ANOTHER KEY RESOURCE:
DOHISTORY (*http://dohistory.org*)

A website called DoHistory (*http://dohistory.org*) models and supports the interactive process of historical inquiry. The site models historical inquiry by investigating the diary entries of Martha Ballard, a midwife in late 18th- and early 19th-century Maine. Materials on the site include digital primary and secondary source text, annotated images, and graphic organizers (see Figure 7.3).

The site models historical inquiry through guided practice. Although some structure and interpretation are provided, the inquiry depends on the interaction of users to work through and make meaning from background and primary source documents. Users can choose one of two "research topics" and delve deeper into Martha Ballard's diary through an online version of the diary. The site provides users with an initial overview and background information, which they can investigate more fully through links to primary sources and accompanying questions to clarify main ideas. Then, at each stage of the investigation, users can access digital versions of primary source documents and search the online diary. Interactive exercises in transcribing, decoding, and using a "magic lens" to transcribe a handwritten page from Martha Ballard's diary provide more guided practice and support in learning the skills of a historian.

The site supports users in conducting independent historical inquiry with a History Toolkit: guides for stages of historical research, for working with different types of primary sources (including handwritten sources), and probing questions to ask when approaching any historical source.

Because this site provides extensive guidance and models, including "half-full" exercises, it robustly supports students in learning what historical research with primary sources looks like, how to use a variety of primary source documents, and how to conduct historical inquiry themselves.

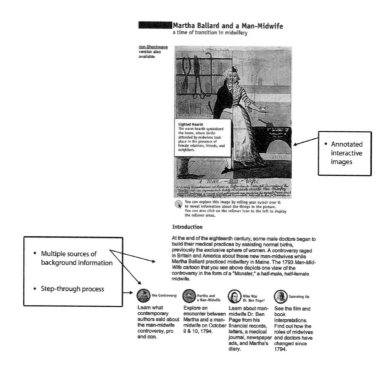

FIGURE 7.3. "Martha Ballard and a Man-Midwife." Do History. *http://dohistory.org/man-midwife/index.html.* Copyright 2000 by President and Fellows of Harvard College. Reprinted with permission from the Roy Rosenzweig Center for History and New Media, George Mason University.

primary source documents, as well as learning the vocabulary of historical inquiry. The glossary support is available only on an as-needed basis, and many students may not require it. But *all* students have the option to use the glossary support when and where they need it. For students who are ready to do so, the glossary can be a chance to create their own multimedia definitions for words unfamiliar to them.

Coaches provide further support for historical inquiry and comprehension. Advice for what to do, how, and why is available whenever and wherever students choose to access the support. It serves as a scaffold, on an as-needed basis. These flexible, just-in-time supports reinforce teacher instruction in historical inquiry, vocabulary, and comprehension strategies. Built-in flexibility, choices, and supports provide all learners, and especially struggling learners, with the opportunity to participate and succeed in the curriculum.

The *Making History* example demonstrates the flexibility of web-based digital learning to meet diverse needs and interests. This and other flexible materials facilitate Doing History the UDL way. But materials are only one piece of the puzzle. Teaching methods need to be tuned to both the Doing History and UDL framework and strategies.

Methods

Within the UDL framework, what are some instructional methods teachers can use to facilitate student understanding, skills, and engagement with Doing History? Instructional methods that reflect UDL are those that are flexible enough—*from the start*—to support diverse students in engaging with, understanding, organizing, and acting upon information. In this context, effective teaching requires a shift from the traditional "stand and deliver" model, where teachers convey key information and students receive and learn. To enable students to develop their own inquiry skills sufficiently to become expert learners and practitioners of historical inquiry, the classroom needs to be more like an apprenticeship environment than a traditional classroom. Keys to creating such an environment are modeling, supported practice, ongoing feedback, collaboration, and increasing independence.

The digital UDL environment supports teaching strategies and methods supported by research in the Doing History approach. For example, research shows greater learning when teachers *make thinking visible, provide background knowledge and connections to students' current lives, and provide support for vocabulary understanding and development.* In this section, we highlight some examples of how the principles of UDL and Doing History align.

Such approaches to teaching are supported by the digital environment, because the materials themselves can provide supports that previously required a teacher's involvement. With the help of embedded supports such as TTS capability, on-screen coaching, and linked vocabulary, students have more independence. In addition, teachers can focus their work where it is most needed and where they are most effective—working with individuals or small groups to develop historical inquiry skills.

Research shows that teaching historical inquiry requires *making historical thinking visible* to learners by providing prompts, think-alouds, models, and mentoring to support students in developing historical skills and understanding (Greenleaf, Schoenbach, Cziko, & Mueller, 2001). When the dynamic process of making meaning is made visible for students, and when students are supported in "digging in" to make meaning from sources themselves, social studies and history are reclaimed as active cognitive enterprises. As students become more expert in the "how" of history, they become better at understanding the "what" (the content) of history. With support, all students, particularly struggling learners, can benefit from this dynamic approach to social studies and history learning.

In a UDL-based learning environment, the kinds of support provided can change as students' skills and understanding grow. Teachers serve as mentors and guides in the process of inquiry, and students, like any other apprentices, begin at a novice stage in which they need a significant amount of guidance, modeling, explicit think-alouds, tools, and other supports provided by the expert mentors (both the on-screen coaches and, more importantly, the teacher). Teachers model skills for students, with the aim to make the hidden processes of analytical thinking visible; they show students what successful learners do to read and understand. Students then apply these techniques to their own exploration of historical documents and periodically reflect on their own thought processes through personal reflection or metacognitive conversations. Taking notes either in text or via audio recording helps students think about how they are learning in addition to what they are learning, and how different types of documents require different skills. Doing this challenging metacognitive work helps students explore who they are as learners, what strengths they bring to the learning tasks, and what strategies they can use to handle challenging texts (Greenleaf et al., 2001; Palincsar & Brown, 1984).

Another priority for teachers of inquiry-based history is to *provide background knowledge,* so that students can see how what they are about to learn relates both to what they already know and to other historical events. In UDL-based history instruction, some basic background knowledge can be embedded in the materials, to be accessed by students when and where they need extra information. This frees the teacher to build the critical background knowledge actively with students. Activating and developing background knowledge *with* students encourages the students to explore what they already know and to make connections with their own lives, concerns, and priorities. Background-building activities also enable teachers to assess what their students already know and do not know, correct misconceptions, and decide where instruction needs to fill in gaps in student knowledge and understanding.

Providing vocabulary support is also essential. Before students can analyze a document and use it effectively in historical inquiry, they must be able to read and comprehend what the document says. Historical documents can be particularly difficult to read because of dated vocabulary. As students work with more primary sources, it becomes even more critical to bridge the gap between the students' current vocabulary and the vocabulary of the past.

UDL AND THE EXEMPLARY HUMAN BEING PROJECT

Christine Draper is a middle school social studies teacher whose classes include high-achieving, typical, and struggling learners. Each fall, she has her seventh-grade students do the "Exemplary Human Being Project," an inquiry-based research project.

The project begins as Dr. Draper introduces the project goals: to identify, research, and report on an exemplary person. To begin the process, the class has a group discussion about the word "exemplary." Who does it mean? What are some examples of exemplary persons the group can think of? What makes these people exemplary?

Next, students think about themselves and the kinds of persons they want to become. What characteristics do they want to exemplify? After students record their personal exemplary qualities in the project rubric, they begin research to find a person who exemplifies these qualities. Students choose their own sources and can choose a variety of these, including print text and web-based sources, for their research.

Each student produces a finished product for the project consisting of a persuasive essay and a visual presentation. The process of creating the persuasive essay is robustly supported during the project. Students use the project rubric to guide writing and self-monitoring. A model of proficient performance and a rubric with clearly defined criteria for success are also included. In addition to the rubric, students use WPP Online, a writing practice program that provides feedback on writing mechanics, clarity, main ideas and supporting details. After generating their first drafts and evaluating these through WPP Online, students self-evaluate their essays: They highlight main ideas, note supporting details, and annotate revisions that they identify during the self-evaluation. At the end of the project, each student turns in all materials, including the rubric, drafts, and finished essay, to Dr. Draper.

Each student also creates a visual presentation as an artifact of the research. Students have a choices in what to create for the visual presentation: a poster, a painting, a poem, a sculpture, a model, a collage, a short video, a PowerPoint or HyperStudio presentation, a website, or a mobile. The rubric also gives the criteria for a successful visual presentation for the Exemplary Human Being Project.

Students check in with Dr. Draper during each stage of this 3-week assignment, providing her with opportunities to monitor their progress, correct any misconceptions, and help them meet challenges in comprehension and action/expression. Each student's final grade for the project is based on the completed rubric, annotated drafts, the final draft of the persuasive essay, and the visual presentation.

The Exemplary Human Being Project provides one example of applying UDL to a lesson's goals, methods, materials, and assessments. The lesson offers learners flexibility, choice, and support in how they complete the project. Dr. Draper defines and models the goal and the multiple means of achieving the goal. Flexible methods include teacher-guided discussion, student–teacher conferences, self-evaluations, and supports that leverage technical tools (such as WPP Online) to provide students with ongoing feedback. Materials are not limited in any way; students find and use the sources they find most valuable. Assessment is ongoing and formative through conferences and self-evaluation, and the final grade is a compilation of performance during inquiry and in two different modalities of artifacts.

Research on vocabulary support and comprehension shows that when teachers explain meaning of challenging words in student-friendly terms and give students the opportunity to work with and make words their own, student vocabulary knowledge and comprehension of reading material increase (Beck, McKeown, & Kucan, 2002).

In a digital environment, several approaches can be used to support students for whom arcane words are a barrier. One is to create a glossary, using student-friendly language, images, and audio to define, explain, and illustrate usage for terms in ways students will understand. Another is to offer a modern version of the text in which arcane words are replaced with their modern equivalents. Remember, the goal is for students to understand the sources, not to master Olde English! Beyond supports that can be embedded in the materials, teachers can model thinking and working with words: They can explain and demonstrate how they seek out the meaning of words that are hard for them, and how they express these words in a way that makes sense to them. Students can then practice creating their own "student-friendly" definitions as a group, and can even build their own glossaries for individual or shared group use. Or, after modeling the conversion of an arcane document into modern language, teachers can ask groups of students to create their own modern versions of primary sources that interest them.

A UDL approach to historical inquiry shifts teachers' role and methods from one in which the teachers are the experts imparting information to students, to a mentoring model wherein teachers prompt, guide, and support learners. Technology supports students and teachers in this change, and assists all learners in reaching a greater understanding of the past. Flexible digital materials enable teachers to offer more options to students in terms of choosing documents, accessing background knowledge, and supporting vocabulary development and comprehension of events; all these options enable learners to focus more closely on the process of Doing History itself. Teachers, in turn, are freed from lecturing and become collaborators with students in an apprenticeship model of learning, which focuses more on guiding learners in growing in the skills and understanding of the historical inquiry process.

None of these tools and techniques will enable students to become experts in historical inquiry without assessments that are meaningful and appropriate. How does assessment look when a class is Doing History the UDL way?

Assessment

Frequent monitoring of students' progress toward learning goals is also a key element of UDL. Teacher and student knowledge of progress is important for sustaining motivation and engagement, as well as addressing challenges before they become frustrating. In UDL-based history instruction, students are given clear goals and criteria for success, choices of topics and materials, models of proficient performance, and choices for how to express their understanding. Assessment should reflect these practices likewise. The goals and criteria for successful achievement of those goals will be clear from the beginning of the unit, and assessment should be based on those goals.

Of course, assessment should be ongoing as well as summative. For ongoing assessment, the artifacts a student produces in a unit and over the school year provide a record of progress in skill and understanding; these artifacts can be used to create a multidimensional picture of student understanding. Digital learning environments lend themselves to embedded ongoing assessment. For example, students can use a digital graphic organizer with structured questions to help them organize their notes and viewpoints on diverse primary sources. Or students can respond to embedded prompts to help them practice discipline-specific strategies, such as locating, corroborating, and evaluating sources. In reviewing students' ongoing notes and responses, teachers can make course corrections, offering either more support or challenges to keep students engaged.

In *Making History*, learners are presented with an outline of the historical inquiry process as they begin their inquiry project. This outline makes the process that students are responsible for mastering clear and transparent, and students are supported in executing these steps as they work through the inquiry project. As students work, they reflect on their progress with this outline and through short conferences with their teachers at each step of the process. These conferences enable teachers and students to gauge how they are doing, where they are particularly strong, and when they may need additional support. In the end, students' grades will not be a surprise, because they have been involved with evaluating their own progress throughout the project.

UDL-based instruction involves providing students with choices, supports, and scaffolds, and creating curriculum materials that are flexible enough to support the diversity of learners in today's classrooms. Effective assessment uses these same principles to accurately gauge students' understanding and skills. In assessing students' understanding of concepts and mastery of skills, the most authentic assessment environment will use the same flexible UDL environment in which students learned. In short, the form of the assessment should match the form of instruction.

Although it may seem counterintuitive to offer supports such as TTS or glossary support when evaluating a student, it is important to remember the learning goal and to align the means of assessing students with that goal. Providing support that is noncriterial (i.e., support that does not assist students *directly* in the skill or knowledge being assessed) will only produce a more accurate idea of whether the students have actually mastered the task. Thus if some students can best demonstrate their ability to evaluate and synthesize sources to create a strong argument by using a video, oral, or art presentation, these options should be offered. An analogy could be made to having students with motor problems learn to write essays with a word processor, and then asking them to handwrite their responses on an exam. This would certainly not tap into their optimal performance in composition!

Similarly, UDL-based summative (end-of-unit) assessment should give students these same options and supports they had during instruction when these do not interfere with the skill and content being assessed. For example, if the assessment is meant to measure understanding of the causes of the Boston Massacre, students can be given a choice in how to express that understanding; some will choose to write, while others will create oral or visual documents that show their understanding. Unless the ability to recall information in a specific, limited time period is part of the skill assessed, students should have the option of working on summative assessments outside the formal classroom setting.

CONCLUSION

We want students to develop a broad understanding of the past, as well as the skills to critically evaluate the world that surrounds them today. Recent research shows that students learn best when they are actively engaged and motivated in the process of learning. In order for students to deeply understand historical events and develop inquiry skills, they need to participate actively in making meaning from primary source documents.

The Doing History approach, when designed according to UDL principles, offers a framework for supporting students in understanding what they learn, how they learn, and why they should invest their time and energy in these challenging tasks. Engagement and motivation are particularly important for students who struggle with learning. Although Doing History is an exciting method of guiding students in learning these skills and gaining understanding, historical documents present barriers to many students; learners need support and guidance on how to make meaning from the disparate information presented in primary source materials.

Using a UDL approach with flexible digital materials and tools makes Doing History even more powerful and effective for highly diverse learners. Students gain access to a wider variety of documents, and can access and understand these documents through embedded decoding and comprehension supports. UDL environments also greatly enhance teachers' ability to offer supported, flexible ways for students to express their growing understanding and skills. In part because students can work more independently, teachers can now focus on students' interests and act as guides and mentors, collaborating with students as they gain in understanding and skills. Moreover, as teachers support students in learning vocabulary, comprehension strategies, and historical inquiry skills, they empower students to take control of their learning and develop lifelong critical thinking skills for making meaning in any context.

REFERENCES

Beck, I., McKeown, M., & Gromoll, E. (1989). Learning from social studies text. *Cognition and Instruction, 6,* 99–158.

Beck, I., McKeown, M., & Kucan, L. (2002). *Bringing words to life: Robust vocabulary instruction.* New York: Guilford Press.

De La Paz, S. (2005). Effects of historical reasoning instruction and writing strategy mastery in culturally and academically diverse middle school classrooms. *Journal of Educational Psychology, 97*(2), 139–156.

Gabella, M. (1994). Beyond the looking glass: Bringing students into the conversation of historical inquiry. *Theory and Research in Social Education, 22*(3), 340–363.

Greenleaf, C., Schoenbach, R., Cziko, C., & Mueller, F. (2001). Apprenticing adolescent readers to academic literacy. *Harvard Educational Review, 71*(1), 79–129.

Levstik, L., & Barton, K. (2011). *Doing history: Investigating with children in elementary and middle schools* (4th ed.). New York: Routledge.

National Center for Education Statistics. (2002). *The nation's report card: U.S. history 2001* (NCES 2002-483). Washington, DC: Author.

National Center for Education Statistics. (2007). *The nation's report card: U.S. history 2006* (NCES 20007-474). Washington, DC: Author.

Palincsar, A. S., & Brown, A. (1984). Reciprocal teaching of comprehension-fostering and comprehension-monitoring activities. *Cognition and Instruction, 1*(2), 117–175.

Robinson, K. (2010). *Making history: A guided exploration of historical inquiry.* Teacher edition retrieved from *http://bookbuilder.cast.org/view.php?op=model&book=11209&page=1*; student edition retrieved from *http://bookbuilder.cast.org/view.php?op=view&book=11209&page=1*.

Rose, D., & Meyer, A. (2002). *Teaching every student in the digital age: Universal Design for Learning.* Alexandria, VA: Association for Supervision and Curriculum Development.

Saye, J. W., & Brush, T. (2006). Comparing teachers' strategies for supporting student inquiry in a problem-based multimedia-enhanced history unit. *Theory and Research in Social Education, 34*(2), 183–212.

Seixas, P. (1993). The community of inquiry as a basis for knowledge and learning: The case of history. *American Educational Research Journal, 30*(2), 305–324.

Spoehr, K. T., & Spoehr, L. W. (1994). Learning to think historically. *Educational Psychologist, 29*(2), 207–222.

Stahl, S. A., Hynd, C. R., Britton, B., K., McNish, M. M., & Bosquet, D. (1996). What happens when students read multiple source documents in history? *Reading Research Quarterly, 31*, 430–456.

VanSledright, B. (2002). Confronting history's interpretive paradox while teaching fifth graders to investigate the past. *American Educational Research Journal, 39*(4), 1089–1115.

Wineburg, S. S. (1991). On the reading of historical texts: Notes on the breach between school and academy. *American Educational Research Journal, 28*, 495–519.

Wineburg, S. (2001). *Historical thinking and other unnatural acts: Charting the future of teaching the past.* Philadelphia: Temple University Press.

CHAPTER 8

Universal Design for Learning and the Arts Option

DON GLASS, KATI BLAIR, and PATRICIA GANLEY

As classrooms in America's schools have become more inclusive over the past quarter-century, general education classrooms now include students with a broad range of cultures, home languages, experiences, and abilities. The process of inclusion requires educators to widen learning opportunities and options to support these many kinds of learners in integrated settings. The knowledge and practices of Universal Design for Learning (UDL) will help educators provide multiple and flexible options for enabling a variety of students to access and engage with content, as well as to demonstrate their understanding, knowledge, and skills. The arts can play a powerful role in enhancing these options.

Part of the process of UDL implementation is providing engaging and relevant content with flexible low- and high-tech tools to support various pathways to learning. We also need to make a transition in our thinking as educators—from retrofitting modifications in response to particular disabilities of students or groups of students, to designing learning opportunities and spaces from the beginning that are more universal. That is, we need to remove curricular barriers to make options available to all students. We authors suggest that this process requires the core principles of excellence and access, as well as a problem-solving orientation. CAST's (2011) UDL principles, Guidelines, checkpoints prompt our thinking in this direction.

In this chapter, we explore the UDL framework for arts instruction, using three case examples from classrooms. First, however, we provide some context by discussing the critical features of the arts teaching and learning option.

THE ARTS OPTION

At the core, we educators must always maintain high expectations and standards for all students. We do this by designing-high quality, challenging, meaningful, and accessible curriculum and instruction with multiple opportunities for all students to be engaged and successful in achieving common learning outcomes. Building on knowledge from the special education field and the standards and equity movement, Dennie Palmer Wolf (2008) argues that including dimensions from the arts will enable us to expand our definitions of excellence and access not only in the arts, but in many fields of learning. In this chapter, we build on this argument by demonstrating how the arts can provide particularly rich, meaningful, and engaging teaching and learning options for a range of students. We use three examples drawn from a range of arts disciplines as illustrations.

The arts can provide engaging multimodal alternatives for the representation of content and for meaningful expression and action. For example, the arts can provide rich creative teaching and learning opportunities that align with what Newmann, Lopez, and Bryk (1998) call high-quality intellectual work—knowledge construction, disciplined inquiry, and applications beyond school. Using the materials and processes of art can provide students with opportunities to engage in culture and meaning making. The arts often require disciplined guided and independent practice; the exploration and application of skills and ideas; and elaborated communication of ideas, meaning, and purpose. Often the arts involve products or performances similar to those that are expected in the world of creative work (e.g., completed visual artwork or craft objects, public performances, film or media, design models, etc.).

As we will see in the first two case examples, the arts can also provide options for exploring content that integrate well with other subject areas. "Arts integration," or the interdisciplinary connections between arts skills/knowledge and other subject areas, has been a curricular focus in the arts education field (Burnaford, Brown, Doherty, & McLaughlin, 2007). Part of this attraction seems to come from how the arts—particularly contemporary forms of the arts—are focused on using various media to explore concepts that help us to understand our personal and cultural selves and communities. We argue here that the arts provide a particularly rich and engaging set of tools and processes to explore "big ideas" (Chaille, 2008) and "essential understandings" (Wiggins & McTighe, 1998) of worthwhile content that connect with the lives of young people.

The arts allow for instructional options across many of the UDL Guidelines and checkpoints, as well as the possibility of engaging many supporting neural networks. For example, teaching the arts can provide additional multimodal opportunities for content to be represented, which relates to the brain's recognition networks. Furthermore, the arts provide opportunities for nonlinguistically and crosslinguistically representing information, symbolism, and metaphor, using a wide range of forms. Students can engage with and demonstrate their understanding of content in a variety of media (spoken words, literature, theater, film and mixed media, visual or sculptural images, music, sound, etc.). This represents a shift from concentrating on the arts as a subject area to emphasizing the arts as a learning strategy (Glass, 2010).

DANCE AND MOVEMENT OPTIONS

In this first example, we illustrate how a teaching artist, a general education teacher, and a special education teacher collaborated to design an inclusive language arts unit of study that was integrated with dance and movement.

Identifying and Removing Barriers

The students in this example had a wide range of abilities, but they were working to meet the same learning goals. At the start of the collaboration, teaching artist Marsha Parrilla sat with the teachers at a table introducing the concepts of dance, while learning about the teachers' curricular goals. Four of the students used wheelchairs; some had limited mobility; one student had low vision; another student verbally echoed responses that were not always connected to the task; and one student had a possible hearing impairment. Half of the students had been identified as English language learners. Although the discussion started with the students' needs and strengths, it moved into identifying learning outcomes, curricular barriers, and UDL solutions.

Together, they decided that the broad goal of comprehending text would guide the collaboration. Typically, students have opportunities through whole-group instruction, questions and answers, individual reading, and writing to engage in and express what they understand from text. This collaboration was unique, in that a teaching artist introduced dance processes that provided options for students to engage with and demonstrate what they comprehended from the text. The lesson provided opportunities for students to become dancers, choreographers, and audience members as part of their response to literature (see Table 8.1).

Starting with Language Arts

The session described in this example was targeted to help students make predictions about what would happen next in a story, and explain why their predictions were confirmed or disconfirmed (CAST, 2009). To begin the lesson, Marsha sat in front of the entire group of students and read the book *Not a Box* by Antoinette Portis (2006). In the text, the main character is asked why he is sitting in, standing on, spraying, or wearing a box. Each time, he insists, "It's not a box!" and the opposite page reveals the many things he imagines his cardboard box to be: a race car, a mountain, a burning building, a robot. As Marsha read the book, the students made predictions about what the main character is imagining as he remakes his cardboard box.

TABLE 8.1. UDL Options Added to the Literacy Unit by Integrating Dance and Movement

Multiple means of representation (Principle I)	Multiple means of action and expression (Principle II)	Multiple means of engagement (Principle III)
Checkpoint 2.5: Provide options that illustrate key concepts through multiple media. The teaching artist increases students' access to content through the use of different sensory modalities. For example, the teaching artist reads the story aloud and uses illustrations to build comprehension. *Checkpoint 3.2*: Provide options that highlight patterns, critical features, big ideas, and relationships. In addition to the read-aloud and illustrations, the teaching artist uses guiding prompt questions to highlight the critical features of the curriculum: prediction and imagination.	*Checkpoint 4.1*: Provide options in the mode of physical response. In the movement exercises, the teaching artist provides alternative options for the students to respond to literature. *Checkpoint 5.1*: Provide options in the media for communication. The teaching artist offers multiple ways for the students to compose—through speech, music, movement, and dance.	*Checkpoint 7.1*: Provide options that increase individual choice and autonomy. The teaching artist gives students the choice in the kinds of movements to use for their collaborative machines and cool-down. *Checkpoint 8.3*: Provide options that foster collaboration and community. The teaching artist has students work in small groups to build on each other's movements. This requires collaboration and community to make sure that the machine parts integrate well as a whole and that the meanings of the movements are aligned with the function of the machine.

After reading the text, Marsha asked the students what the main character is doing with the box. The students responded that he is imagining. Then Marsha explained that imagining was what they would do today during her visit to the school. To make the transition from reading and listening to movement, Marsha played soothing music and led the students in a series of warm-up movements.

Integrating Movement and Dance Options

Marsha then asked a fellow teacher to build a set of movements with her. Marsha moved her arms back and forth with her hands clasped, and then invited the teacher to add to this movement. The two teachers moved in reaction to each other. Marsha asked the students, "What kind of machine are we?" The purpose of this was to engage students in imagining what machine the teachers could be, based on their movements. Students were then asked to explain their responses. This modeling demonstrated the role performers would have in making and sharing their creations, and also showed how to be an active audience member who interpreted meaning based on observational evidence.

From here, students were divided into small groups of four to five, and they began to create a moving machine or a moving operation of their own. Each student in the group made a part of the machine with his or her body, and the group moved together to perform a working machine. They were individual and group choreographers making an image with their movements. The students created an original idea and found ways to communicate their idea to their peers in a collaborative manner.

As each group performed, the audience members took an active role in observing, describing, and interpreting the movements that they saw. They observed the performance and predicted the function of each machine, based on details that they saw in the movements. In this dialogue, the makers of each dance were able to hear how their peers interpreted their movements.

The audience members then heard directly from the dance makers why their predictions were correct or not, as well as what machine the group intended the movements to portray. This exercise extended the act of imagination into a process of creation, interpretation, and communication. The general and special education teachers continued the dance exercises during weekly literature lessons, giving the students an opportunity to access comprehension and communication through their bodies.

VISUAL ARTS OPTIONS

This section features an inclusive unit of study for middle school students that integrated and enhanced learning outcomes in both language arts and visual literacy.

Identifying and Overcoming Barriers

By the time they reach the middle grades, students are expected to "read to learn," not "learn to read." Basic reading skills are not taught as a part of the standard curriculum. The learning focus is on synthesis of information, composition, and gaining a wider knowledge of the world through literature. However, large numbers of students find it challenging to read grade-level text. A barrier to learning in schools today is often the "disconnect" between the tasks assigned to students and the purposes of learning particular skills or information. In the context of high-stakes testing, state and federal mandates, and required curricula, students rarely have an opportunity for their voices to be heard. The students in this classroom were moved by what they had learned about the Holocaust and felt they had important things to say. Given the opportunity to publish their thoughts, they were engaged and invested in finding powerful vehicles to communicate.

Another barrier for students, and for many people in general, in creating visual art is their belief that they are not "artists"—that they cannot draw, paint, or sculpt, and therefore cannot generate images that can communicate a strong message. The biggest barrier for students participating in the visual elements lesson was their belief that they were not capable of creating art. However, when images were broken down into simple, understandable elements, it became clear that everyone could produce interesting, powerful art. When students understood these visual elements, they were able to use visual media confidently and competently to communicate ideas, concepts, and feelings.

Starting with Language Arts

The language arts teacher utilized a web-based, universally designed, digital reading environment to make sure that her students were able to access and understand the novels in their unit on the Holocaust. The web-based environment included text-to-speech software; vocabulary and background information; and embedded reciprocal teaching comprehension prompts and supports for students (i.e., predicting, questioning, summarizing, clarifying, making connections, and visualizing while reading or listening to the text).

In the digital environment, students had the options of responding to prompts by using the keyboard or by making audio recordings. Digital logs of student work allowed the teacher to view and respond to students in real time, and allowed the students to review and revise their work. All of these UDL and accessibility features allowed the diverse classroom of students to participate in the language arts curriculum, fully immerse themselves in the stories of the adolescent characters, and understand the horror of living in Europe during this time in history.

The learning goals derived from the state language arts standards included literature and writing language arts composition, as well as making connections and response to literature. Using multimedia to communicate ideas was an overlapping learning goal of each area in the standards.

Using the visualization responses from their logs, students created poems in the style of their choice. Students demonstrated their knowledge of process and genre through writing "author's notes." The poems were powerful and vivid depictions of the characters and of the emotions students experienced while reading the novels. The following is an example of a poem that a student generated as part of this unit of study:

Not Me

Lonely, cold. Nazi
is part of me. I
am a stranger to
myself.
TRAITOR
Who knows why?
Not me. Not me.

NOT ME.
I feel
empty and heartless.
Destroying my
motherland.
This person really isn't me.
My heart is
dying.
Frozen,
shattered.
No.
This is not me.
I am gone . . .

Integrating Visual Arts Options

Inspired by the quality of their work, the teacher and class wanted to share their work and learning with the larger community. Inspired by *I Never Saw Another Butterfly* (Volavková, 1993), a book of illustrated poetry by children living in the Terezin concentration camp during World War II, they decided to create and publish their own anthology. They also decided to create images to accompany their poetry. The challenge was for all the students to produce images that were as powerful as the poetry that they created—images that communicated the emotions and intensity of their writing.

Using a projector, the teacher began the lesson by focusing on examples of color as the basic building block of visual literacy. The lesson continued by showing well-known abstract paintings, especially those of Georgia O'Keeffe, and having the class observe and evaluate how the carefully selected color and shapes used by the artists communicated specific moods and emotions. O'Keeffe's *Wall with Green Door*, a painting consisting of soft, warm beige and green squares and rectangles, evoked feelings of safe contentment. Her *Black White and Blue*, consisting primarily of dark, geometric, hard-edged shapes, suggested a gloomy or dangerous atmosphere to the class.

Symbols in the artwork and in the politics of the time, like swastikas, crosses, flags, doves, doorways, roads, and light versus dark, were discussed. The class continued to look at paintings to practice identifying the visual elements and their use in communicating the artists' intent. Students then reread their poems to remind them of the emotions they wanted to communicate. Students made decisions about the visual elements, especially color, shape, and symbolism, for their images.

The visual arts learning outcome was for students to understand and demonstrate knowledge of basic visual elements, color, shape, and use of symbolism. Assessment of the outcome was based on the image each student produced, along with an artist's note that explained his or her creative process. The resulting images and text were sophisticated and compelling (Figures 8.1–8.3).

FIGURE 8.1. *Artist's note:* "My illustration is called *Dark Moaning*. I have the darkest color black with red. The black stands for the dark and sickening minds of the Nazis. The red stands for the bloodshed in the war and the anger the people were seeing and feeling their own family dying each day by Nazis' guns or by hunger."

FIGURE 8.2. *Artist's note:* "I made an abstract oil pastel/watercolor piece because it reflects the dark mood of the poem. The watercolors behind the pastels show darkness filling all the light left. I also like how you could blend the oil pastels together to create a specific look. The black heart represents the traitor's choice to desert his country, and the dim faded background represents what was once his life, but has now faded into oblivion."

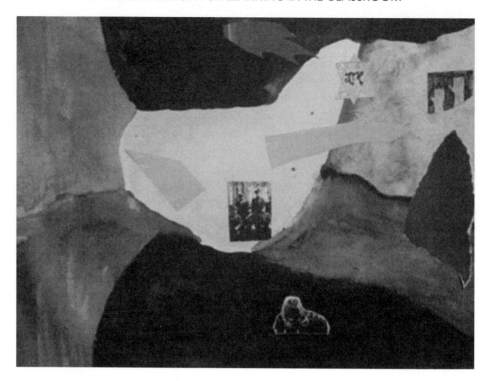

FIGURE 8.3. *Artist's note:* "When I did my artwork I tried to capture a few different things. The lighter colors represent where the Jews are and the one route that they can take to escape. That's why I called my picture 'Escape.' The solid shapes represent the people who would help them on their journey to freedom and away from the Nazis who loom in the dark colors. The photos of people show how they lived in the different sections The Jewish Star I wanted to represent them passing the boundaries of the Nazis and being free. The hands represent the helping hands that helped them on their way to be free. Finally, to tie in with my poem, I wanted to add several colors that were not [too] dark to represent the Nazi soldiers who caved in and allowed people like Pieter and the dog to live."

UDL Solutions

In the Holocaust unit, the flexibility of the materials, methods, and assessments allowed all students to participate and attain high levels of competence. Looking at the unit and the lesson through the UDL lens, we can identify the principles that supported the diverse learners in the middle school language arts classroom.

Providing "multiple means of representation" (UDL Principle I) and options for comprehension gave students a choice of reading or listening to text. Embedded comprehension supports helped students understand and immerse themselves in powerful, grade-level novels. The universally designed reading environment also provided vocabulary support and highlighted key concepts.

Providing "multiple means of action and expression" (UDL Principle II) in the reading environment meant that students could choose to type or audio-record their responses to the reciprocal reading strategies. They had access to multiple levels of support to respond to the reading prompts, as well as support for executive functioning through practice and feedback from the teacher. In the visual elements lesson, there was time to practice identifying and analyzing the visual elements. Students explored and analyzed the paintings of celebrated artists as models for their own work.

Providing "multiple means of engagement" (UDL Principle III) occurred throughout the unit. Engagement was key to the success of this unit. Because all students could access the literature, they were transformed by it. Everyone—those whose first language was not English, those with reading disabilities, those with vision impairment, those who had never successfully completed reading a novel— were able to share and participate in the knowledge and discussions. Publishing their work provided further motivation to learn new skills and exert effort toward the goal.[1]

MUSIC OPTIONS

Our third case example features a classroom that used multiple flexible options to engage young people in making music. Instrumental music programs are typically provided to students who attend extra hours of school or are pulled out during the school day for weekly instruction. Teaching artist and music educator Tim Archibald saw an opportunity to create a different kind of instrumental program as he worked to build a fully inclusive instrumental music class for all third, fourth, and fifth graders at the Henderson School in Boston, Massachusetts.

Identifying and Removing Barriers

Tim began the program by using xylophones. He applied colored labels to each bar to guide students to play the notes and to provide additional visual support. The xylophones engaged most students, but still presented barriers to some students. Several students became overstimulated by the sound of other students playing their xylophones together. To others, the design of the mallet presented a physical barrier to playing music. In addition, the colored labels did not help students with blindness or low vision. With no built-in support to help students know what note to strike at any given time, many students could not stay engaged long enough to learn songs on the xylophone. Reading musical notation presented a barrier for many as well. The initial attempt at including all students did not work, but what Tim learned through the process gave him a better understanding of the barriers present in traditional instrumental programs.

---

[1]To see more UDL options for units of study exploring the Holocaust, see the essay by Wolf (2008), with a case example by Molloy and Rodriguez (2008).

UDL Solutions

Tim soon became an expert at seeing where and when students encountered barriers as they learned how to play an instrument. At the Henderson School, students are taught to be self-advocates. They can tell you what they need in order to learn or participate with their peers. This culture allows students and teachers to identify and address barriers collaboratively.

Armed with this knowledge, Tim continued to look for solutions and finally discovered a set of keyboards equipped with technology that would provide various levels of support, challenge, and opportunities for self-assessment. Using the keyboards not only removed many of the barriers presented by traditional instruments, but allowed students to develop skills individually with scaffolded supports and headphones before attempting to play as an ensemble. By including this new tool with his multisensory approach to teaching, Tim provided more students with an opportunity to play an instrument.

> You [can] stand next to a student using the headphones and be able to understand what they are getting, and also what supports they may need from you. You can get this feedback in a very quick, individualized way instead of having to have some type of assessment or some type of playing test. That's huge. It really makes it easy to get one-on-one with a larger group of students.
>
> —TIM ARCHIBALD

Providing Multiple, Flexible Options for Students

The following is a description of a typical keyboard class with Tim at the Henderson School. This example illustrates the flexibility and choice provided in both the presentation of instruction and the actions students engaged in during the keyboard class.

Tim began the class with all students seated on the floor to review musical scales and the song they were currently working on, "When the Saints Go Marching In." Tim used a set of stairs from the stage to show how notes go up and down, just as we go up and down stairs. The stairs were numbered to correspond to the notes that were numbered on the keyboards. As a volunteer played Note 1, Tim asked a student volunteer to ascend to Step 1. The student walked up the stairs as the volunteer played the notes up the scale. This helped students understand both kinesthetically and visually how notes go up and down the musical scale. Tim also illustrated this concept by drawing the notes on a scale with the help of students. Students thus had a low-tech visual, auditory, and physical representation of the musical scale.

Students then selected from three keyboard options and combinations to suit their level of supports and challenges: visual cues, auditory cues, and tempo adjustments. For example, students who were blind could choose to play along with just auditory cues. To extend their learning, students could also choose to play the song independently without any of the supports provided by the keyboards. In addition, students could increase their performance levels by attempting to play the piano with other classmates.

Providing Ongoing, Responsive Feedback

Throughout the class, Tim saw a wide range of performance levels. When some students quickly moved through the levels, while others sat focused on one level for the entire class, persisting in order to increase their abilities in terms of tempo or fingering. Tim constantly jumped from keyboard to keyboard, to provide each individual with support to increase his or her engagement. When some students needed help hearing a rest in the music, he animated the concept of the rest in music with his body. When others needed help with tempo, he asked them to vocalize the tempo with him as they fingered the song along with the keyboard prompts.

Along with the supports that Tim provided during the class, the keyboards provided feedback to students; flexibility is a major advantage of these keyboards. Students could monitor their progress as they played a song through a score given to them by the keyboards. Students could also choose when they were playing to be evaluated or when they were just practicing. When they chose to be evaluated, the keyboards measured their progress and instantly reported a number on the screen. The keyboards also lit up as a reward for high scores. Tim mentioned that this feature had really increased the students' engagement. For the students, it became similar to improving their performance in a video game.

Students sometimes shared their scores in joy and disappointment. Because the keyboards gave a baseline level of feedback to students, Tim had more flexibility to individualize his feedback to students and quickly see whether there was a common challenge that existed in the class. This sharing provided an opportunity for intermittent peer advice and teacher feedback. At the end of the class, students shared their discoveries with the whole group, and Tim asked for volunteers to attempt to play as an ensemble.

> I think that the real joy is when we can all unplug the headphones. We turn them off and play the song together in real time. To be able to play it all together as a group—living and breathing the music—is the ultimate learning outcome. Being able to phrase it together and blend it together— you know, not too loud or not too soft. And even when you make a mistake, the ability to catch back up and to continue is a huge high-order thinking skill when you are operating in real time.
>
> —Tim Archibald

THE UDL GUIDELINES IN PROFESSIONAL DEVELOPMENT

Creating inclusive learning environments is an ongoing process of principled design and action, problem solving, and responsive teaching. The educators profiled in this chapter continue to explore how to provide multiple engaging options and supports for students to develop their executive functioning skills and make self-determined choices about their learning. This ongoing inquiry can and should be collaborative among various educators, paraprofessionals, and school administrators.

In the case examples, we have shown how the UDL Guidelines (CAST, 2011) can play a key role in helping educators and schools move toward universally designed options that identify and remove curricular and instructional barriers. The strengths of the UDL Guidelines are that they are derived from a wide range of experience and practices, are thoroughly grounded in research, and speak to high-quality curriculum and instruction across subject areas. The UDL Guidelines provide a powerful conceptual framework to take the next steps toward really including all students, both those with disabilities and those without.

At VSA, an international association on arts and disability, we have been using the UDL Guidelines as part of our professional development for curriculum design to prompt thinking about expanding learning options for all students. Teaching and learning strategies that may have originally come from modifications for a particular student are reconsidered as options to be made available to everyone by choice. The UDL Guidelines are used in our professional learning communities as a checklist for design and evaluation discussions to see how the arts can provide additional options for learning, and how content can be represented and expressed in a variety of creative ways. As in the case examples in this chapter, the UDL Guidelines are used as an analytic framework to guide ongoing curricular, instructional, and assessment decision making.

CONCLUSION

In this chapter, we have argued that the arts option has the rich potential to extend and enhance the exploration of high-quality content by students in engaging and meaningful ways. We have provided several case examples to show how the arts can provide additional options for representing content and demonstrating understanding, knowledge, and skills though expression and action. We have also shown that making classrooms more inclusive is an ongoing and responsive design process that can be expertly guided by the principles, Guidelines, and checkpoints, of UDL.

REFERENCES

Burnaford, G., Brown, S., Doherty, J., & McLaughlin, J.H. (2007). *Arts integration frameworks, research & practice: A literature review*. Washington, DC: Arts Education Partnership. Retrieved from *http://www.aep-arts.org/files/publications/arts_integration_book_final.pdf*.

CAST. (2009). *VSA arts: The UDL guidelines in teacher professional learning communities*. UDL Spotlight. Retrieved from *http://udlspotlight.wordpress.com/category/vsa-arts*.

CAST. (2011). *Universal Design for Learning Guidelines version 2.0*. Wakefield, MA: Author. Retrieved from *http://www.udlcenter.org/aboutudl/udlguidelines*.

Chaille, C. (2008). *Constructivisim across the curriculum in early childhood classrooms: Big ideas as inspiration*. Boston: Allyn & Bacon.

Glass, D. (2010). The design and evaluation of inclusive arts teaching and learning. In *The contours of inclusion: Inclusive arts teaching and learning.* Washington, DC: VSA. Retrieved from *http://www.eric.ed.gov/ERICWebPortal/detail?accno=ED522677.*

Molloy, T., & Rodriguez, A. (2008). Case example documentation. In *Contours of inclusion: Frameworks and tools for evaluating arts in education.* Washington, DC: VSA. Retrieved from *http://www.eric.ed.gov/ERICWebPortal/detail?accno=ED507539.*

Newmann, F. M., Lopez, G., & Bryk, A. S. (1998). *The quality of intellectual work in Chicago schools: A baseline report.* Chicago: Consortium for Chicago School Research. Retrieved from *http://ccsr.uchicago.edu/publications/p0f04.pdf.*

Portis, A. (2006). *Not a box.* New York: HarperCollins.

Volavková, H. (Ed.). (1993). *I never saw another butterfly* (expanded 2nd ed.). New York: Schocken Books.

Wiggins, G., & McTighe, J. (1998). *Understanding by design.* Alexandria, VA: Association for Supervision and Curriculum Development.

Wolf, D. P. (2008). Building and evaluating "freedom machines": When is arts education a setting for equitable learning? In *Contours of inclusion: Frameworks and tools for evaluating arts in education.* Washington, DC: VSA. Retrieved from *http://www.eric.ed.gov/ERICWeb-Portal/detail?accno=ED507539.*

CHAPTER 9

Universal Design for Learning "Unplugged"

Applications in Low-Tech Settings

DAVID H. ROSE, JENNA W. GRAVEL, and YVONNE DOMINGS

One of the most basic and persistent questions about Universal Design for Learning (UDL) is this: "Can I do UDL well without a lot of modern technology?" It is an important question for several reasons. First, from a practical standpoint, many teachers who are attracted to UDL *as an idea* are unsure whether they can actually *implement* it, in view of their limited access to technology or their limited fluency in its use. Second, from a theoretical standpoint, many educators have asked whether technology is central to the foundations of UDL or whether UDL is useful as a pedagogical framework that goes beyond technology. Starkly put, is UDL about technology, or about teaching?

In this chapter we address these questions directly, using the UDL Guidelines as a structural framework. Our exploration will reveal that while modern technology is important in the implementation and elaboration of UDL, the UDL principles and Guidelines may be applied for successful teaching of *all* students, even without modern technologies.

We do not claim that it is better to implement UDL without modern technology. Quite the contrary is true. From the beginning, UDL has been associated with modern technology for good reason: The power and flexibility of modern technology greatly enhance the ability to individualize and customize the learning experience. Whereas older fixed technologies, like print, demanded standardized approaches to teaching and learning, the newer technologies allow and even encourage flexibility and diversity instead. Yet we hope to reveal in this chapter that UDL sets out principles that are focused on teaching and learning, not on the technologies—either ancient or modern—with which those principles are realized.

THE PRINCIPLES OF UDL

As mentioned throughout this book, the three basic principles of UDL (Rose & Meyer, 2002), are these:

I. Provide multiple means of representation ("what" we teach and learn).
II. Provide multiple means of action and expression ("how" we teach and learn).
III. Provide multiple means of engagement ("why" we teach and learn).

The UDL Guidelines (CAST, 2011; see Lapinski, Gravel, & Rose, Chapter 2, this volume) are based on these three principles and provide a framework for identifying the ways in which students differ, as well as for identifying specific evidence-based options and alternatives to consider in designing successful learning activities for all students. In the following pages, we use these Guidelines, and the best UDL practices they recommend, to structure our discussion.

AN EXAMPLE LESSON: THE SEED LESSON

To provide focus, we choose a single lesson—one that uses essentially no technology and is familiar to most elementary school teachers—to reexamine the foundations of UDL and its guidelines:

This lesson helps students understand and articulate the life cycle of plants. Begin by cutting open a few different types of fruits and vegetables to reveal the seeds. Show the students some dried seed pods. Put all of these examples on tables around the room, and encourage students to explore the way the seeds look, feel, smell, or sound. Provide students with magnifying glasses and checklists of features for which they should be looking. Once students have the opportunity to explore, ask the students to sort the seeds and dried seed pods into groups. Also ask them to record their observations in a journal through words or drawings. Students can help label the seeds that they can identify, and you can work together to create a seed museum. Encourage them to collect seeds or seed pods at home and bring them in for the seed museum. During reading time, allow students to pick from several different books to read about the life cycle of plants. Put out materials for planting seeds. Include a variety of seeds that are fairly fast-growing, like sunflowers or beans. Explain and model the planting process. Have a wall chart that lists the steps of the process in text and in pictures, and also have a word wall to display all of the new vocabulary associated with the lesson. Subsequently, all of the students can plant their own seeds in plant boxes near the windows (or outside if weather and space permit), and can record the progress over the next few weeks in their journals—in words, in drawings, in pictures, in simple graphs or charts. If conditions allow, follow the plants to maturity, harvest their seeds, add them to the museum, and reflect on the full life cycle of plants.

Principle I: Provide Multiple Means of Representation

The Seed Lesson, like almost any learning activity, contains information that is essential for the learner. Such information may have many purposes—to inform, to guide, to explain, to prompt, to support, to provide feedback, to extrapolate. None of those purposes can be achieved equitably if the information is inaccessible to some or all of the students.

Whether the information achieves its purpose depends partly on its content—whether the information is accurate, complete, authoritative, organized—but also on how it is presented, or represented. To be effective, information must be represented in an appropriate medium for its purpose and in an appropriate medium for its audience.

From a UDL perspective, it is assumed that there is no single way to present information so that it can achieve both of these objectives. That is, there is no single way to represent information so that (1) it will reach all members of a diverse audience equally well, and (2) it will represent all types of information equally well. Instead, UDL calls for options in the means of representation, so that it can be effective across the full spectrum of what is to be learned, as well as across the full spectrum of learners.

But what kinds of options are needed? The guidelines for representation recognize three broad kinds of options: (1) sensory/perceptual options; (2) linguistic options; and (3) cognitive options. Together, these three kinds of options address most or all of the challenges that differing students typically face, and that differing information demands. We consider each of these in turn.

Guideline 1: Provide Options for Perception

From a UDL perspective, the Seed Lesson has a "natural" advantage: Its information is accessible through multiple sensory modalities. Children can learn about the growth of seeds and plants by looking at them, touching them, tasting them, smelling them, and even perhaps hearing them. By contrast, presenting the same lesson in a traditional workbook or textbook would narrow the information channel to only one modality—vision. There are two very negative consequences of that narrowing: There are fewer things to learn, and fewer ways to learn them.

Let us expand those points briefly. First, because a workbook or textbook presents information only visually, it allows fewer ways to access and learn the information about seeds and plants. For example, students with many different kinds of visual impairments—blindness, color blindness, low vision, visual agnosia—would find the information in the textbook wholly or substantially inaccessible. (There are many other students for whom the textbook rendering of the Seed Lesson would be linguistically or cognitively inaccessible, and we consider them in the sections ahead. Here we are considering only the sensory accessibility of the lesson.) In the Seed Lesson, on the other hand, there are alternative routes to the information: through various aspects of touch (e.g., shape, size, texture, hardness, temperature, etc.), as well as through smell, taste, or hearing (e.g., shaking and manipulating the plants or seeds).

Just as importantly, the narrowing of sensory modalities would impose another impediment: There are fewer things to learn—for any student—in the textbook version. Many properties of seeds and plants, or any other aspects of the world we live in, cannot be adequately represented or learned through vision. The smell of daffodils, onions, or basil; the texture of cotton; the taste of sour lemon or maple sugar are all properties and distinctions of plants that cannot be rendered visually. From a UDL perspective, or even from a developmental or cultural perspective, the reduction in sensory properties is a reduction in access to knowledge. Moreover, reading about seeds rather than exploring them and experimenting with them is a reduction in access to the ways of knowing that we call "science."

Guideline 2: Provide Options for Language, Mathematical Expressions, and Symbols

Although the Seed Lesson is rich in direct sensory/perceptual experiences, much of its actual instruction depends upon the information conveyed through language and symbols. Throughout the lesson, the teacher uses his or her own language—both spoken and written—to inform, elaborate, emphasize, guide, clarify, give feedback, and reflect. Moreover, the teacher is not the only source of critical language in this lesson; the observations, questions, and explanations (as well as the tone and contagious verbal enthusiasm!) of other students in the lesson are important elements of how the learning is initiated and extended.

But not all students are equally facile with the teacher's language. For some, this language is not their primary language at all. Others differ widely in their linguistic abilities and disabilities—in the breadth and depth of their vocabulary development, their syntactic ability, their knowledge of idioms and expressions, their ability to extract language from written text (reading), and many other aspects of the language used for instruction.

Fortunately, the Seed Lesson incorporates many aspects of the UDL Guidelines for language, expressions, and symbols. These options provide critical access routes for some students, and enrich the language-learning opportunities for many. Let us consider here just one aspect of the language being used (and addressed in the Guidelines)—vocabulary.

One of the major barriers to acquiring information through language is the mastery of the vocabulary that it requires. Students are highly diverse in any or all of the domains of vocabulary: the vocabulary that their families use at home, the vocabulary that the dominant culture in the community uses, the vocabulary that is used in this particular school setting, and the domain-specific vocabulary (in this case, the vocabulary of science, biology, or ecology).

Instructionally, the first instinct is often to "dumb the vocabulary down"—to reduce the general level of vocabulary to a "lowest common denominator," and/or to limit the introduction of new vocabulary so that it is accessible to even the most struggling of students. This is generally not the best option. All children, from the most linguistically advanced to the most linguistically limited, need to continue their overall vocabulary development aggressively—and that development is not encouraged when rich vocabulary is reduced or eliminated from instruction. Furthermore, the development of domain-specific vocabulary (vocabulary about seeds, plants, and biology, in our case) is often crucial to building competence in the new domain of knowledge. New words, and the concepts they stand for, are often the structural foundations that guide students in "what to look for" and "what to learn."

For those reasons, optimal instruction consistently incorporates rich and expanding vocabulary. But the Seed Lesson provides multiple options that support students in learning from language, even those students who have the weakest foundation for acquiring new words.

From the outset, note that new vocabulary in the Seed Lesson is introduced and embedded in a meaningful activity, rich in a relevant, authentic context that cognitive science has shown will scaffold the recognition, acquisition, and recall of new vocabulary much better than isolated "vocabulary-building" tasks or dictionary look-up exercises. The Seed Lesson also inherently illustrates concepts through multiple media (e.g., the physical seeds, plants, and tools themselves)—one of the key "multiple representations" of vocabulary suggested in the UDL Guidelines.

But for some students, such supports will not be sufficient. The teacher provides others, such as the classroom "word wall" and student-created dictionaries on vocabulary posters that are prominently displayed during and after the lesson. These options, and others included in the UDL Guidelines, are designed to "smarten up" vocabulary development, not "dumb it down."

It is important to reflect on one important point. Many lessons are difficult to comprehend (and thus to learn) because they use *too much* language when other forms of representation would be more effective. The UDL framework reminds educators to illustrate through multiple media for two reasons. First, for some students in any classroom, language is an imperfect or disabling medium. Second, many things worth learning are not conveyed most directly or cogently through language at all. Much of the knowledge in the Seed Lesson is accessible through direct exploration and experimentation, which are especially good methods to use in a lesson based in science.

Guideline 3: Provide Options for Comprehension

In the Seed Lesson, when the teacher passes out a checklist to guide the students in what to look for, he or she is scaffolding their comprehension. More specifically, the teacher is using one of the options recommended within UDL Guideline 3: a scaffold designed to "guide information processing, visualization, and manipulation." What does that mean?

When faced with a task like the observation of the Seed Lesson, experienced learners use prior knowledge to facilitate their learning of new information. That is, because of what they have learned earlier, they know what to look for, how to focus their attention, and how to find the features that are most distinctive. Lacking that experience, many students attend to a great deal of information that is irrelevant, redundant, or unimportant. By providing the checklist, the teacher is using his or her own prior learning as a scaffold to guide the students' information processing.

Given the diversity in any classroom, the UDL Guidelines recommend providing some options in checklists—including, for example, a checklist that is very challenging and can be used to guide the most inquisitive and knowledgeable of students. Even graduate students and seasoned scholars in science—from botany to anthropology—benefit from such observational checklists. Providing checklists at several different levels of complexity maximizes the chance that all students, from the most inexperienced to the most advanced, will find the challenges and supports they need.

The Seed Lesson includes another option to "guide information processing" that we would like to highlight. Expert learners differ from novices not only in the amount of prior information and experience they bring to new learning, but in the availability of active strategies and skills that they can apply—strategies for systemically exploring new information, strategies for organizing the new information and comparing it to old, and strategies for intentionally remembering new information (mnemonic strategies), to name only a few. Effective teachers continually model such strategies, making their thinking visible for their students. In the Seed Lesson, for example, the teacher could begin by modeling or "thinking aloud" for the students while demonstrating what to do. For example, the teacher might say, "When I first look at a plant in order to tell what kind of plant it is, I first look at the leaves. I look to see what kind of overall shape they have—how round they are, how pointy they are, how wide or narrow they are. Here, help me look at this leaf. What do you see?" Such modeling and mentoring are important scaffolding options for apprentices in any domain.

The Seed Lesson also illustrates another Guideline 3 option for scaffolding comprehension: "Highlight patterns, critical features, big ideas, and relationships." Most teachers point out the distinctive parts of a seed or plant; draw attention to the features distinguishing this particular plant from another (e.g., the pattern of the leaves, the height of the stem, the size and shape of the seeds); or use a magnifying glass to emphasize the distinctive vein structure of the leaves. But the lesson has other, more active options for highlighting critical features. The "seed museum," and the accompanying activities of identifying, comparing, labeling, and sorting seeds, are perfect for highlighting critical features. By engaging in these activities, students also begin to learn a great deal about categories, relationships, and even taxonomies. An advantage of this option is that there are actually many ways to sort seeds (e.g., by their color, density, volume, species), which vary widely in their level of complexity. As a result, each student can approach the task and participate fully, but at an appropriate level of challenge.

The comprehension-scaffolding options we have described here are all examples of representing information in multiple ways. Their value is not limited to merely making lessons more accessible, but extends to providing the apprentice-ships in knowledge building that every student needs.

Principle II: Provide Multiple Means of Action and Expression

Not only do students need to build knowledge; they also need to learn how to express that knowledge effectively. The UDL framework emphasizes, therefore, the critical importance of providing a wide range of expressive options. The narrow range of options typically found in most classrooms has two disadvantages: There are fewer forms of expression to learn, and fewer ways to learn them. Let us con-sider these two points briefly.

First, there are huge individual differences among students in their capabil-ity for any particular means of action or expression. What is an optimal means of expression for one student may be an ineffective or even impossible means for another. As a result, the UDL Guidelines stress the importance of separating means from ends. Every student should have high expectations or goals for expression, but the means for achieving those goals may, and should, differ. Moreover, in the development of skills, what is an optimal next step for one student may be far too difficult for another, and far too elementary or boring for yet another. As a result, the UDL Guidelines remind educators to consider options that scaffold learners appropriately at different levels of expertise—from beginner to expert—so that all learners are both supported and challenged as they learn.

Second, there are differences in what each medium of instruction can express effectively. Too often schools concentrate on only a few forms of expression, primar-ily written expression. But in the real world, communication increasingly demands literacy in a much more diverse palette of media: text, images, video, sound, recorded movement, simulation, and so forth. In this new world, the concentration on written expression alone leaves students underprepared for their futures.

To meet both challenges—the challenge of individual diversity, and the chal-lenge of literacy in more diverse media—the UDL Guidelines provide a framework for expanding the expressive options in the classroom. They encourage educators to consider broader expressive options in three categories: options in the motor and physical demands for expression, in the specific media used for expression and communication, and in the executive and organizational requirements for expres-sion. Let us consider these options in turn.

Guideline 4: Provide Options for Physical Action

In most school-based learning experiences, the only required physical activity is turning pages in a book or writing with a pencil or pen. The Seed Lesson, however, requires modest motor activity: physically sorting seeds into categories, prepar-ing the soil for planting, digging holes or furrows, carrying and then dispensing water or fertilizer, staking and tying up tall plants as they grow, and so forth. None of these are particularly challenging for most students, but they impose special challenges for some, particularly those with physical and motor disabilities. Is that a good thing or a bad thing?

That depends, and here is where it is critical to be very clear about the goal of the lesson. It is often assumed that the best way to make this lesson accessible is to reduce or eliminate its motor and physical demands. From a UDL perspective, however, it is better to provide options in the ways to meet the challenge, thereby helping students to develop a rich array of strategies. Indeed, the Seed Lesson, with appropriate "options for physical action," can provide just the right kinds of learning opportunities for students with motor or physical disabilities—opportunities that are difficult to create in isolated physical or occupational therapy sessions. It is precisely because the Seed Lesson inherently requires physical action, motor coordination, and even dexterity that it is valuable, especially to students with physical and motor disabilities.

What is important, however, is to provide sufficient options. To ensure that all students can participate in learning from the physical demands of any activity, the UDL Guidelines suggest two kinds of options. We consider one of these kinds: optimizing access to tools and assistive technologies.

One of the advantages of the Seed Lesson is that most of its activities require special tools (the magnifying glass, a shovel or trowel, a hose or watering can, string or other fasteners, etc.). All of these tools extend human capacity, and learning how to use them is an important part of becoming competent in our culture. The UDL Guidelines remind us that students with motor disabilities will need the same thing. With the help of specialists, like the school occupational therapist or physical therapist, effective tools appropriate to the Seed Lesson can be provided even for individuals with the most severe disabilities. For hand tools, there are specially designed versions that have "easy grips," special releases, and other features that have been carefully designed (in many cases, universally designed) to augment the capacities of individuals with a wide range of physical abilities.

What is important about providing these options is that they are precisely the kinds of options that students with physical disabilities need to master as they prepare for their future lives. The best way for them to learn to choose and use tools is not in isolated therapy sessions but in authentic tasks where, with careful mentoring and support, they can learn to augment their own capacities in an organized and instructional way. Removing the natural challenges of the Seed Lesson does not prepare them for their future, whereas providing opportunities to practice with new tools will.

Guideline 5: Provide Options for Expression and Communication

In the Seed Lesson, students are asked to record and chart the progress of their plants in their journals. An important strength of this lesson is that it offers "options for expression and communication" in doing so. Among other options, the lesson provides "multiple *media* for communication." Students are encouraged to represent and communicate what they observe "in words, in drawings, in pictures, in simple graphs or charts." Providing such options has many educational advantages: It allows students to learn to use the best medium for what needs to be expressed; it allows individual students to find alternatives that are optimal for their own strengths and weaknesses; and it allows teachers to assess more accurately what each student has learned.

But such media options also raise an important concern about UDL. If students have many options to express themselves, will they ever develop the difficult skills with which they struggle? All students, but especially those who struggle as writers, need to continue to learn to write. They will never become better writers if they don't practice writing. The central dilemma is this: How can struggling writers participate fully in high-level content-area lessons, like the Seed Lesson, and yet also participate in the extended remedial practice they need to improve their writing? From a UDL perspective, the solution will be familiar: Provide options in the ways that students write. But what kinds of options should be provided?

The kinds of options that can be helpful are highlighted in the UDL Guidelines under "Build fluencies with graduated levels of support for practice and performance." To be fluent is to be able to do something smoothly and with ease. This could apply to any number of skills in schools, such as speaking, reading, and writing, but it could also be extended to include expression in any kind of media. Some students will need little or no scaffolding because their basic skills are already fluent and well developed. Others will need considerable scaffolding to continue to participate meaningfully. Diverse options will be needed to meet the challenges of diverse individuals.

Within the Seed Lesson, it is easy to imagine diverse levels of scaffolding. In an environment where students use their computers for writing, many helpful scaffolds are available—from spell checkers and grammar checkers to word prediction and interactive concept maps. In the Seed Lesson as described, however, the teacher already provides a number of helpful non- or low-technology scaffolding options. For example, the word wall provides both semantic and spelling support for the apprentice writer. The checklists that are designed to help students know what to look for in their observations can double as organizers or "reminders" to structure their writing. In addition, teachers can also provide (either directly in student journals, or as supplementary guides or templates) many structural supports to help students get started and organize their thoughts: sentence starters, structural templates that break down the writing into sections, concept maps, and so forth. And of course, both teachers and peers can provide key scaffolding opportunities.

Providing these options for scaffolding within the Seed Lesson actually serves the two very different purposes that are often in conflict for teachers. First, students who struggle with basic skills can participate more fully in the actual science of the Seed Lesson. Second, those same students can find the graduated apprenticeship in writing that they need to develop their basic skills. The scaffolding options that give struggling writers a better chance to engage fully in science writing can also allow them the opportunities they need to practice and develop as writers.

Guideline 6: Provide Options for Executive Functions

One of the most demanding aspects of the Seed Lesson is almost completely hidden or implicit: its requirements for executive functions. "Executive functions" are defined as the system of cognitive processes that control and manage other cognitive processes—a group of processes that are responsible for strategy, planning, and regulating behavior. To participate in the lesson, all students, to some extent, have to act like executives: They have to set (or adopt) various goals during their participation, plan sequences of actions or activities, organize their resources, and monitor their progress. Young children, like those for whom the Seed Lesson is intended, have very little capacity for such executive functions. Indeed, modern neuroscience has shown that the areas of the brain most responsible for such functions do not reach maturity until late in adolescence or adulthood.

As a result, every culture recognizes the need to provide external scaffolding and support for executive functions during childhood. Children are not considered independent executives, but are highly dependent on teachers or parents, the structure provided by the curriculum, and the external organization of the classroom activities or environment. When students are much older, they will be expected to have internalized these "executive functions" so that they can act independently, but certainly not yet. And, of course, there is great variability among students in their capabilities for executive function at any age.

Fortunately, the Seed Lesson already provides a great deal of external scaffolding. In fact, it is likely that many aspects of the scaffolding are immediately apparent as one enters the classroom: It is organized into distinctive functional areas, each with appropriate resources and tools; there are topic-related charts, diagrams, and models on the walls; and there are schedules and routines on whiteboards or easels. Each of these features provides external support for executive functions. Students at this age are not, for example, prepared to manage and organize a great deal of information independently; their working memory capacity is far more limited than that of older students. The UDL Guidelines recommend providing options to "facilitate managing information and resources," because such options are critical for all young students, but also for many older students as well. From middle school upward, one of the primary sources of variance among students is in their ability to exercise these executive or "metacognitive" abilities—those abilities that prepare them for effective extended problem solving and communication. Particularly vulnerable are students with learning disabilities and students who are young or novices in a domain. These students typically seem immature, disorganized, forgetful, unprepared—weak in all of the executive capacities. Effective teachers provide options in the classroom that can help such students. The wall charts and diagrams described earlier constitute one type of scaffold that reduces the working memory load, essentially supplementing internal capacity with external capacity by helping students "hold" the required information while they are learning. Many other options are typically recommended to help students retain and organize information. The best are those that prepare them for productivity in their lives ahead:

providing graphic organizers and templates for recording information, teaching students how to take notes and keep their notes in organized folders, and so forth.

Without such external supports, students are often mistakenly assumed to lack content-specific knowledge or skills, or are assumed to be unmotivated or unengaged. Instead, what they lack are the executive skills or strategies to organize and express that knowledge effectively. They often fail to complete assignments in a timely fashion; submit disorganized projects; or otherwise perform poorly in activities that demand organization, planning, and progress monitoring. When those executive or organizational skills are not central to the lesson's goals, many students will achieve better results and learn more when options for executive functions are available.

Principle III: Provide Multiple Means of Engagement

If cognition is the vehicle for constructing knowledge from information, then motivation is its engine. Researchers and theorists in many branches of the learning sciences have increasingly recognized the critical role of emotion and motivation in any constructive learning. Information that does not engage a learner, that is not actively attended to, is rarely transformed into knowledge.

Information that does not engage a student's attention is in fact inaccessible. It is inaccessible both in the moment (relevant information goes unnoticed and unprocessed) and in the future (relevant information is unlikely to be remembered). Knowing this, teachers devote considerable effort to increasing students' attention and engagement. But students differ significantly in what attracts their attention and engages their interest. Even the same students differ over time and circumstance: Their interests change as they develop and gain new knowledge and skills, and as they differentiate into self-determined adolescents and adults. Therefore, it is essential to offer alternative ways to recruit student interest—ways that reflect important inter- and intraindividual learner differences.

Typical classrooms offer very few options and opportunities for engagement. Students are treated as if they are all the same. These limited options and opportunities for engagement result in two negative consequences: There are fewer ways to motivate students, and fewer ways for students to learn how to motivate themselves. Let us reexamine the Seed Lesson from an engagement standpoint.

Guideline 7: Provide Options for Recruiting Interest

The Seed Lesson begins with an "attention grabber"—a ripe, colorful, juicy fruit to explore. The fruit is both familiar (students recognize its look, feel, and smell) and also unexpected (school lessons don't usually begin with anything that is actually juicy or tasty). By beginning the lesson in this way, the teacher hopes to engage the students in learning—to attract their attention to the lesson, and away from the vast array of other things that might engage them.

Such recruiting of interest is one of the most challenging tasks in teaching. There are two challenges, in fact. On the one hand, there is the challenge of recruiting interest in *learning* per se. Many extrinsic rewards capture attention, for example, but the attraction is to the seductive quality of the reward itself—what is sometimes called "eye candy"—rather than to the goal of learning. On the other hand, there is the challenge of individual differences. Students are as diverse in what interests or engages them as they are in any other aspect of learning; the best way to recruit the interest of one student may be ineffective or off-putting to another.

To meet these challenges, UDL Guideline 7 recommends several kinds of options. We consider one—providing options that "minimize threats and distractions." In the Seed Lesson, the teacher seeks to create a learning environment in which all students feel safe. As described above, gradually releasable scaffolds are embedded into the lesson, to ensure that students feel just the right amount of support and challenge to make them feel secure and comfortable. Yet the Seed Lesson also extends this guideline in a way that we think is highly effective. The teacher not only *minimizes* certain threats and distractions, but strives to *vary* others. Why is varying threats and distractions also a productive strategy? Why might a teacher ever want to have threats and distractions in the classroom? The answer to this question goes to the very heart of UDL.

The Seed Lesson begins by encouraging students to explore the ways the fruits, vegetables, and seeds look, feel, smell, and sound. For many of the students, diving deeply into the flesh of a tomato or pumpkin to find its seeds is highly engaging; the messier and juicier, the better. There are inevitably some, however, who are hesitant to engage in that way. At the extreme of the distribution are students "on the spectrum" (those with autism or Asperger's syndrome) or students with tactile defensiveness, who often find such novel and immersive sensory experiences overstimulating, even threatening. Trying to recruit their interest in this way may erect a barrier rather than a ramp to learning. A UDL approach encourages these options: allowing such students to watch other students (or the teacher) from a respectful distance; encouraging some students (or their parents) to help prepare for the activity by trying it under less stimulating conditions at home first; providing a template of the activity with pictures or illustrations of the steps to make it more predictable; or providing an opportunity to conduct the exploration in a safe setting.

This example may seem extreme, but the difficulty is very common. For many students (including, for instance, those labeled as "shy"), many activities designed to build engagement—brainstorming as a group, putting on a public demonstration or performance, acting in a play, or relating personally relevant anecdotes—are not engaging at all, but are threatening or distracting. The job of educators, however, is not to create an artificial environment where such threats and distractions do not exist, but to provide sufficient options for all children—starting from where they are—to learn how to cope with the distractions and threats that will be inevitable ahead. Our challenge is to prepare students to live in the world as it is.

Guideline 8: Provide Options for Sustaining Effort and Persistence

Once engaged, many students find the Seed Lesson sufficiently compelling to interest them in learning about the resources their plant will need to thrive. For others, the long cycle of waiting for their plant to mature, or the added burden of keeping a journal or portfolio of their plant's development, or repeatedly measuring and graphing their plant's growth, may tax their patience, endurance, and commitment.

UDL Guideline 8 recommends several kinds of options to support the sustained effort and persistence necessary to complete this (or any other) project. As with other guidelines, there are two reasons for doing so: (1) to meet the challenge of diversity among students in their existing abilities to sustain such effort and persistence; and (2) to provide the instructional scaffolds needed so that all students can practice and develop higher-level strategies that they can eventually use on their own.

Guideline 8 recommends four kinds of options: options that heighten the salience of goals and objectives; options that vary demands and resources to optimize challenge; options that foster collaboration and community; and options that increase mastery-oriented feedback. We examine the first of these.

An advantage of the Seed Lesson is that its goal is consistently explicit, constantly available, and highly "salient." The developing plants are highly visible and constant reminders of the primary learning objective: an understanding that plants need resources to grow. If students forget or get distracted by other activities, the plants themselves will begin to wilt—making explicit their requirements for water, sunlight, and nutrients. Equally important, they serve as physical reminders to the students, not only of their need for resources but also of the students' goal to provide them. This may seem trivial, but for many activities in classrooms the goal either is implicit or was made explicit only at the beginning of the activity. For some students in any activity, and for all students in particularly protracted activities, sustained effort and engagement require periodic or persistent reminders not only of the goal, but also of its importance or value.

For young students and novices, these reminders must be extrinsic, provided by their mentors or the environment. But it is important for them to learn how to internalize the process: how to remind themselves of their goals so that they can ultimately reach them; how to periodically revisualize their goals and their rewards, to maintain motivation and persistence in spite of difficulties; how to keep their goals salient in the face of many attractive distractions. The UDL Guidelines recommend multiple scaffolding options (with opportunity for gradual release of the scaffolds) so that every child can have an optimal apprenticeship that leads to independence.

Guideline 9: Provide Options for Self-Regulation

The focus of the Seed Lesson is on plant biology. But every lesson in school, every activity, is an important opportunity for students to continue their long apprenticeship toward emotional maturity—what is often called "self-regulation." Individual students differ significantly in their needs for developing self-regulation. Some students need primarily to learn to manage the anxiety that comes with engaging in anything new, such as the novel or social aspects of the Seed Lesson. For others, the primary goal may be to learn to manage the frustrations that come from the obstacles and disappointments in the long project of growing seeds into plants. For yet others, the primary goal may be to learn how to collaborate with other students in group projects without either dominating or rejecting them. To reach any of these goals, students will need extended apprenticeships with options or scaffolds that can help guide and support each of them appropriately.

UDL Guideline 9 recommends three kinds of options for self-regulation: options that promote expectations and beliefs that optimize motivation; options that facilitate personal coping skills and strategies; and options that develop self-assessment and reflection. We briefly examine one of these.

Imagine a teacher preparing for a particularly collaborative aspect of the Seed Lesson. Knowing that most of the students are novices in the kinds of self-regulation that collaboration will require, and that there are some students with particular difficulties in this area, the teacher prepares options ahead of time. Knowing that one key aspect of self-regulation is the ability to monitor one's own performance, the teacher provides options to "develop self-assessment and reflection."

Specifically, the teacher begins the group work by handing each student a rubric for evaluating his or her own participation in the collaboration. Such rubrics are very common in education, from kindergarten through graduate school, precisely because they enable novices in learning to evaluate and reflect on their own participation. This rubric is very simple, with a single criterion and only four levels of response:

- Level 1: Arguing or not doing anything to help the group.
- Level 2: Working in the same group, but working alone.
- Level 3: Working cooperatively with one other group member.
- Level 4: Everyone has a job, and the group is working cooperatively.

With this simple rubric as a scaffold, even the most inexperienced students can begin to reflect on their own performance. As they learn to be proficient at that first step, the teacher can expand the rubric so that it guides and challenges more effective monitoring and self-control. By differentiating the level of the rubric to each student's existing level of performance, the teacher can ensure that every child is sufficiently and appropriately challenged to grow. In this small way, the Seed Lesson provides a natural opportunity to prepare students for their future—a future in which monitoring their own behavior is one key aspect of successful self-regulation.

CONCLUSION

We have begun this chapter with a simple question: Can UDL be implemented without modern technology? Our examination of the Seed Lesson illustrates that most or all of the UDL Guidelines and benchmarks can be admirably implemented without any particular technology at all. What UDL *does* require—and this is critical—is a well-designed lesson from the start. And a well-designed lesson is one that is constructed to offer sufficient options (in both challenges and supports) that all of its learners will be successful. Although designing a lesson with sufficient options for all students is certainly more challenging without the flexibility and additional power of modern technology, it is important to take advantage of the UDL approach, whether there is any technology or not. Technology is not the goal of UDL; it is merely one of its means.

And that is the most important point of this chapter: UDL is not primarily about technology; it is about pedagogy. The most radical aspect of UDL is not that it raises our expectations about technology, but that it raises our expectations about education. Whereas traditional education sets low expectations for many students and tends to see them as too disabled, too disadvantaged, or too diverse to make adequate yearly progress, UDL raises a radically different expectation: that it is our curricula that are too disabled, too disadvantaged, or too uniform to reach goals that really matter. UDL provides an approach, based on the sciences of learning rather than the sciences of technology, for designing learning environments that have high expectations—and results—for *all* students.

REFERENCES

CAST. (2011). *Universal Design for Learning Guidelines version 2.0.* Wakefield, MA: Author. Retrieved February 23, 2012, from *http://www.udlcenter.org/aboutudl/udlguidelines.*

Rose, D. H., & Meyer, A. (2002). *Teaching every student in the digital age: Universal Design for Learning.* Alexandria, VA: Association for Supervision and Curriculum Development.

CHAPTER 10

Preparing Teachers to Implement Universal Design for Learning

Emiliano Ayala, Heather J. Brace, and Skip Stahl

Of all the systemic change initiatives designed to address the diversity in today's classrooms, Universal Design for Learning (UDL) most clearly addresses barriers in the four components of the curriculum itself: its goals, methods, assessments, and materials. Often the general education curriculum and the accountability systems that accompany it are not designed to achieve or measure results for diverse learners, including students with disabilities, English language learners (ELLs), and others. Until very recently, these students have generally not been proactively considered during the planning, design, development, adoption, or validation of the curriculum. As a result, general curricula lack the research-based alternative methods and materials that are needed to instruct and assess diverse learners—and, as a consequence, may create barriers to the learning process.

Traditionally, classroom teachers have addressed diversity by modifying or adapting the curriculum. Most of these adaptations are not systematic, have not been properly based on research, and often abrogate the standards and methods upon which the curriculum was originally based. As a result, they can inadvertently alter the related assessment and accountability systems. Given the increasing need to create more valid educational accountability systems, the general curriculum must be designed from the outset to be accessible to all students; this will eliminate or significantly reduce the myriad modifications that currently exist.

Digital media and the technologies that support students—computers, mobile devices and media players, and high-speed networks—offer great potential for expanding the palette of instruction and providing alternative paths for learning. In the UDL framework, technology can efficiently and accurately provide three things: (1) alternative means of representing information (concepts, etc.)—that is, new methods of access when traditional or initial representations are not accessible or helpful (e.g., spoken, video, or graphic concept maps as alternatives to text); (2) alternative means of expression—that is, alternative means for students to interact with activities and express what they know (e.g., voice input, illustration, composition in alternative media); and (3) alternative means of engagement—that is, more than one means of sustaining effort and motivating students (e.g., varying novelty or the level of challenge).

UDL can reorient teachers' efforts to help diverse students meet similar learning goals by providing flexible instructional materials, techniques, and strategies. The UDL framework and its foundational UDL Guidelines (CAST, 2011) achieve this by providing evidence-based and detailed options for doing these three things:

- Presenting information and content (the "what" of learning).
- Performing tasks and solving problems (the "how" of learning).
- Stimulating interest and attention (the "why" of learning).

A UDL curriculum is designed from the outset to meet the needs of the greatest number of users, minimizing the need for costly, time-consuming, and after-the-fact changes. Although teachers independently cannot institute a complete UDL curriculum, they can become aware of how to identify and minimize curricular barriers that would otherwise impede day-to-day instruction (Rose & Meyer, 2002).

In the following sections, we explore the impact of both the economy and technology on U.S. schools, as well as the inclusion of UDL language in the federal Higher Education Opportunity Act (HEOA) of 2008. We then describe the incorporation of UDL into a California state university's teacher preparation program as a response to that state's growing K–12 diversity.

THE CHANGING AMERICAN CLASSROOM: ONLINE, ANY TIME

To see the future you have to travel on the rough edge of experience.
—HARRIET RUBIN, *Fast Company* magazine (January 2001)

The economic recession that began in late 2007 has led to severe state revenue shortages, which in turn have prompted some states and districts to cut education's expenses while trying to sustain its value. Two cost-cutting measures have emerged as logical applications of the growing availability of digital media and networked technology in schools: the increased use of online education for the delivery of day-to-day instruction, and the replacement of print textbooks with their digital counterparts. Picciano and Seaman (2009) noted that in 2008, over 1 million students were enrolled in K–12 online courses; National Center for Education Statistics data indicated that "on average, students in online learning conditions performed better than those receiving face-to-face instruction" (Means, Toyama, Murphy, Bakia, & Jones,

2009, p. ix). In considering traditional print-based versus technology-enhanced instruction, emerging research in the area of literacy instruction has also shown that in some cases, technology-based UDL approaches to literacy instruction may offer greater literacy gains than traditional text-based approaches may (Coyne, Pisha, Dalton, Zeph, & Cook Smith, 2010). Armed with this empirical evidence, states and districts now view online learning not only as a cost-saving approach, but also as a more effective means of delivering instruction and charting students' progress.

Regardless of a teacher's facility with or preference in regard to online learning, the entire online enterprise is predicated on the use of digital media and tools, which expand the possibilities of UDL. Digital media (text, graphics, video, audio) economize the representation of information in multiple modalities. The online environment offers students multiple means of expression by adding threaded discussion, forum, and/or text chat options. Finally, online learning can engage students in a variety of ways not always available in face-to-face classes by allowing them to choose the time and place of their involvement or the entry point of an instructional sequence.

The shift to digital instructional materials significantly enhances the flexibility of classroom learning resources—a core prerequisite of UDL. Digital content can be used on desktop and laptop computers, less expensive netbooks, and (increasingly) mobile devices like smartphones and media players. Web-based content can be accessed from home as well as from school. All digital curriculum materials are not yet accessible in schools, however, and insufficient attention to this issue may force schools to retrofit or repurchase materials in order to meet the requirements of federal disability, civil rights, and special education statutes. What is the best way to equip teachers to be aware of challenges like the importance of selecting materials that are usable by the greatest array of students? For teacher preparation programs, the reauthorization of the HEOA in 2008 offers some guidance.

The Mandate

The HEOA (Public Law 110-315, August 14, 2008) added specific requirements for all teacher preparation programs (especially those receiving federal funding) related to both UDL and the use of instructional technology. Importantly, the HEOA statute defines UDL and distinguishes "Universal Design for Learning" from "universal design," noting that the latter term emphasizes accessibility only, while the former incorporates accessibility in the service of increasing student achievement.

By way of example, California has incorporated what it calls "Universal Access" into its instructional expectations, in order to address the increased diversity in the state's K–12 student population. As described in more detail in the sections that follow, California is placing greater emphasis on preparing teachers who are skilled at identifying barriers in materials and methods that can limit student achievement. This approach acknowledges that a curriculum must reach students before it can be used to teach them. In all likelihood, teachers entering the classroom during the next 5 years will experience a transition from the present focus on addressing state-specific academic achievement standards to an increased focus on teaching to common core standards. It will be important for novice teachers to understand not only the state and national achievement expectations for their respective age ranges and/or content areas, but also their localized achievement benchmarks and assessments.

The Students

This is a time of increasing diversity in U.S. schools. Students with disabilities are being routinely educated in general education classrooms, and the number of students who are ELLs is steadily rising. The impact of an increased range of student learning potential, cultural and linguistic variations, and socioeconomic discrepancies is nowhere more evident than in the state of California. California is charged with educating not only the most students, but also the most students with disabilities, the largest aggregated group of ELLs, and one of the most racially and culturally divergent student populations in the country. Furthermore, this rich and differentiated assortment of students has emerged rapidly over the past two decades, forcing many changes in educational practice. Teachers entering California schools today face a markedly different student population from that encountered by teachers even as recently as 10 years ago.

Updated federal education statutes, both in general and in special education, will continue to put increased responsibility on classrooms like those in California. In an effort to provide a high-quality education, states like California will need flexibility in providing instruction and materials to a wide range of learners. They will also need flexibility for responding to an increasingly mobile, interconnected, "right here/right now," technology-infused culture that is having an ever greater impact on day-to-day instruction.

Because access to information is nearly ubiquitous, the demands on today's students are markedly different from those on previous generations. The majority of current students are likely to have access to information in almost any discipline, at almost any time. Furthermore, they have nearly immediate access to shared knowledge hubs, and, more importantly, to each other. Increasingly, the role of teachers will be less focused in dispensing information and opinion, and more focused on guiding students in how to learn. As mentioned previously, flexibility will be a key requirement for success, as will the capacity to function comfortably in teaching environment that can be customized for the needs of individual learners. This is the environment anticipated by the UDL framework.

MEETING THE NEEDS OF CALIFORNIA'S CHANGING STUDENT POPULATION

California serves more students in its public schools than any other U.S. state does. During the 2010–2011 academic year, over 6.2 million students were enrolled in K–12 schools statewide, and the growth rate continues to increase (California Department of Education [CDE], 2011). In addition to increasing school enrollment, students who are members of culturally and linguistically diverse groups have dramatically changed the makeup of the typical student body. Whereas culturally and linguistically diverse students accounted for 44% of the student population in 1980, by 2010–2011 this group represented 73%, making California's student population one of the most diverse in the United States (CDE, 2011). These statistics—combined with the facts that approximately one-fourth of California's students are ELLs; special education enrollment has increased 88% in the last 27 years; and over 50% of students qualify for free or reduced-price lunch programs—make it clear that teachers across the state face tremendous challenges in meeting the needs of this growing and diverse student body.

In response, California is focusing on preparing educators to meet the needs of its changing student population. One concept that has received considerable attention in California is "Universal Access." Embedded in state curriculum frameworks and in all general and special educator preparation program standards, Universal Access is a central pedagogical approach that shapes California's vision of how future teachers will support a full range of learners. Universal Access, as defined by the state, is the notion that all students, regardless of their differences, are entitled to access to the curriculum. This fundamental educational equity is accomplished by procuring and/or by designing and implementing inclusive learning materials and environments. For students to benefit from Universal Access, the state acknowledges that teachers need to properly plan instruction, differentiate curriculum, provide specially designed academic instruction in English, and use grouping strategies effectively (Commission on Teacher Credentialing, 2009). Pedagogical strategies that may be useful in planning for Universal Access include progress-monitoring assessments, collaborative planning and organization, differentiation when necessary, employing flexible grouping strategies, and exploring technology or other instructional devices.

PRESERVICE TEACHER PREPARATION: LINKING UNIVERSAL ACCESS TO UDL

Given that California preservice teacher preparation resides primarily within institutions of higher education, each campus is required to address the concept of Universal Access within its program standards and specific course offerings. UDL offers a clear framework that is aligned with the core principles of Universal Access, since the two concepts share a philosophical base. A central tenet of Universal Access is the belief that all students deserve equal access to the core curriculum. This can be accomplished efficiently through effective and flexible instructional design, as well as the increasing use of digital media in the classroom.

Similarly, a core tenet of UDL is the belief that properly designed curricula—ones that promote rich supports for learning and reduce access barriers, while simultaneously maintaining high academic standards—will enable all students to experience greater success. Universal Access, UDL, and the examination of current and emerging educational technologies play an increasingly prominent role at institutions like Sonoma State University (SSU) as they prepare future California teachers to meet their diverse students.

Implementing UDL in Teacher Preparation

The concept of UDL is formally addressed in Collaborative Partnerships and Special Education (EDSP 422), one of the preliminary courses in the SSU teacher preparation program. Course objectives require that preservice teachers demonstrate knowledge of how to organize and manage instruction in order to meet the needs of a full range of learners. Specifically, preservice teachers are provided with opportunities to develop lesson plans where content is made accessible through the use of differentiated instruction.

The EDSP 422 UDL lesson is divided into three distinct phases: (1) UDL Introduction; (2) Structured Discussion and Guided Practice; and (3) UDL Application. Various course components are used to support knowledge and demonstration of UDL principles in practice, including assigned readings; lectures; web-based resources; large- and small-group discussions; and preparation of a sample lesson plan, which incorporates teachers' emerging knowledge of how to apply UDL principles in practice. In both preparation and delivery, the use of UDL in this course mirrors and models UDL practices.

Phase 1: UDL Introduction

Through prior assigned readings and subsequent in-class activities, UDL is framed in terms of the three UDL principles (CAST, 2011; see Lapinski, Gravel, & Rose, Chapter 2, this volume), which emphasize that effective pedagogical practices must include the following:

I. Multiple means of representation, to give students with diverse learning styles various ways of acquiring information and knowledge.

II. Multiple means of action and expression, to provide diverse students with alternatives for demonstrating what they have learned.

III. Multiple means of engagement, to tap into diverse learners' interests, challenge them appropriately, and motivate them to learn.

This framework provides a way for EDSP 422 students to think about how they can proactively create curricula that are flexible in nature and serve to reduce barriers to learning for all students, not just those with special needs. Importantly, they also learn how these guiding principles are directly related to three sets of brain-based learning networks (Rose & Meyer, 2002; Figure 10.1).

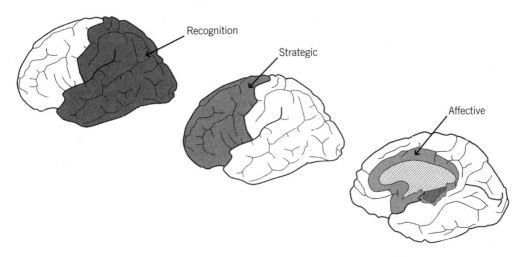

FIGURE 10.1. The UDL principles map onto three sets of brain networks: Recognition, Strategic, and Affective networks. Copyright 2011 by CAST, Inc. All rights reserved. Used with permission.

- Recognition networks—specialized processors designed to receive and analyze information.
- Strategic networks—specialized processors designed to plan and execute action.
- Affective networks—specialized processors designed to evaluate and set priorities.

As noted by CAST (2011), these three sets of neural networks work in unison to acquire, express, and assess the salience of new information and combine it with already acquired knowledge. The three UDL principles are specifically tailored to address the specialized focus of each set of neural networks activated by the learning process. Students also examine how the principles explicitly reinforce the importance of ensuring flexibility in the areas of representation, action/expression, and engagement, in order to address the individual differences present within every student.

Finally, students consider how the use of digital media in support of UDL is preferred, because of the capacity to transform one medium nearly instantly into another (text to speech, image to text, etc.); to provide students with an array of media types (text, audio, video, images, etc.) for expression; and to sustain interest and communication in compelling ways (Rose & Meyer, 2002). This introduction to UDL offers a solid foundation for students as they take some basic steps toward practice.

Phase 2: Structured Discussion and Guided Practice

After a brief review of the prior assigned readings and examination of the UDL foundations discussed above, EDSP 422 students are assigned to small groups where they work collaboratively to identify appropriate UDL solutions to potential barriers, as well as missed opportunities that may be associated with a traditional lesson plan format. The Examples of UDL Solutions worksheet (*http://www.cast.org/teachingeverystudent/tools/udlsolutionstemplate.cfm*) identifies potential technology-based supports, media, and instructional strategies for each of the three sets of brain-based networks (recognition, strategic, affective) that may minimize barriers to and missed opportunities for learning. Students use this sheet as a guide to create flexible means of representation, action/expression, and engagement within the context of a lesson plan. The sample solutions have a technology-rich focus, which many of the students find extremely beneficial, as these provide accommodations that have not previously been considered. Students are also asked to brainstorm potential barriers and missed opportunities based on their own experiences in the classroom; these provide anchoring points for them as they connect UDL theory to practice.

At this point in the UDL lesson, close examination of the UDL solutions students select are critically examined in light of each student's identified needs. Equally as important, faculty members emphasize to EDSP 422 students that although their UDL solutions have been selected with specific students in mind, their UDL strategies of representation, action/expression, and engagement should be made available to all students. This structured activity enables the students to understand not only how the principles of UDL can affect the way in which individual students learn and process information, but also how UDL can enhance effective pedagogy for all. Finally, it offers them a template to begin exploring the connections among the materials and methods they use to teach, possible barriers or missed opportunities, and (ultimately) possible UDL solutions.

During the large-class share-back, EDSP 422 students are asked to discuss the different UDL solutions they have identified and to provide a rationale for the student-specific and whole-classroom utility of each solution. Critical questions and collaborative discussions are used as means of extending the concept of UDL beyond the walls of the SSU classroom. Given that EDSP 422 students have a wide range of teaching and classroom experience, students are asked to consider the learning characteristics of students, both with and without disabilities, in their own individual classrooms. Given their current classroom experiences, students are asked to respond to the following prompts:

- What are some of the barriers to/breakdowns in student learning?
- What pedagogical approaches/methods are being utilized currently?
- What aspects of UDL might remove those barriers/breakdowns?
- Where would be a good place to start?

Commonly, when an EDSP 422 class is presented with these framing questions, a discussion emerges on the difference between providing accommodations/modifications for individual students and providing whole-classroom UDL practices. The difference between implementing the principles of UDL on an individual versus a classwide basis has been one of the most challenging and enlightening components of the UDL lesson. Many of the students' comments focus on the proactive nature of UDL and the universal utility of the concept not only for students in special education, but also for those in general education. It is important to provide students with compensatory strategies and student-centered activities for learning, as opposed to remediation and passive learning.

Because many of the UDL solutions recommend technologically based strategies, EDSP 422 students often indicate a newfound interest in researching available technologies and their efficacy in the K–12 brain-based learning classroom. Furthermore, students begin to recognize that the UDL framework is an optimal approach, because the entire curriculum (i.e., goals, methods, materials, and assessments) is intentionally and systematically designed from the beginning to address individual differences. Through the in-class activity and associated discussion, preservice teachers learn that the "universal" in UDL does not imply that one solution will work for everyone. It means flexibility and alternatives, not a "one-size-fits-all" procedure.

At this point, UDL is further contextualized for SSU students through a critical examination of various new assumptions surrounding UDL practices:

- Students with disabilities fall along multiple continua of learning differences, rather than in separate categories of disabilities or abilities.
- Typical classes are highly diverse.
- Teacher adjustments benefit all learners, not just those with disabilities.
- The curriculum needs fixing, not the students. That is, instead of remediating students so that they can learn from a set curriculum, the curriculum should be made flexible to accommodate learner differences.
- Curriculum materials must be flexible, varied, and diverse, including digital and online resources, rather than centering on a single textbook.
- Both general education and special education teachers should plan the curriculum (i.e., curriculum planning should capitalize on the collective expertise of both groups of teachers).

During this phase of the discussion, each group is provided with a different assumption and asked to reflect upon the ways in which the principles of UDL address these assumptions. Each group then presents its connections to the larger class, using chart paper to flesh out the group members' ideas. Essentially, the students create a "how-to" outline. These ideas manifest themselves not only in bulleted points, but also in diagrams and pictorial representations of the principles of UDL, including the aforementioned assumptions.

Phase 3: Application

Phases 1 and 2 provide EDSP 422 students with an overview of the UDL model and guided practice in the application of this model to K–12 settings. In Phase 3, these preservice teachers apply what they have learned through class lectures, discussions, and activities to create UDL lesson plans that they will formally implement in their classrooms. That is, to acquire a greater understanding of UDL for the K–12 classroom, each student engages in an independent application activity that involves designing a lesson plan for his or her own classroom use. During this application phase, students have access to the CAST UDL Lesson Builder (*http://lessonbuilder.cast.org*) as a means of scaffolding this transition from theory to practice.

This phase is aligned with the mission of CAST. However, this phase also offers students an orientation to the wealth of resources and materials that are readily available on the CAST websites and intended for educational use. Specifically, the CAST UDL Lesson Builder enables students to (1) review UDL principles and related content, (2) explore model UDL lesson plans, and (3) create their own UDL lesson plans. Students create a log-in that allows them not only to develop their own UDL lesson plans, but also to save and edit them for future use. Students enter information typically associated with traditional lesson plans (overview, standards, goals, methods, plan for assessment, etc.), and the Lesson Builder provides "Help" prompts, where the students can access suggestions for improving their lessons and aligning their methods with the UDL framework.

For example, if students need support in identifying appropriate methods, they are able to click on an icon that provides them with a pop-up box, which then further explains how to identify effective instructional methods. Links to supporting documents such as *Using UDL to Individualize Teaching Methods* (*http://www.cast.org/teachingeverystudent/ideas/tes/chapter6_2.cfm*) where students can learn more about specific methods that support the three principles of UDL, are also provided.

Integration of digital technologies provides preservice teachers with alternative means of both acquiring and presenting content, and K–12 students with options for demonstrating content mastery. Students in EDSP 422 actively explore ways to modify lesson plans according to the UDL Guidelines provided by the National Center on Universal Design for Learning (*http://www.udlcenter.org/aboutudl/udlcurriculum*). These guidelines concretize and expand the UDL principles of representation, action/expression, and by engagement using research-supported examples and curriculum design strategies. Each guideline offers specific checkpoints for reviewing materials and instructional practices, linked to resources and tools for incorporating digital media into instruction (see Figure 10.2 for an example).

Recommendations are provided for each checkpoint as a subentry under the larger guideline and associated UDL principle. These recommendations are important because they expose EDSP 422 students to digital media that have previously been unconsidered. Specifically, in the field of special education, preservice teachers' exposure to digital media has often been limited to assistive technology considerations, which are typically focused on those students with significant disabilities (such as autism, intellectual disabilities, and blindness/deafness). Presenting digital media within the framework of UDL moves preservice teachers beyond this truncated view of assistive technology to include the larger concept of educational technology. Expanding the applicability of technology for students with other disabilities or disadvantages allows EDSP 422 students to realize that digital media yields benefits for all students, not just those with significant disabilities.

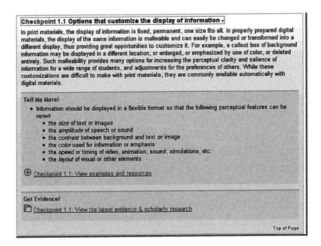

FIGURE 10.2. UDL Guidelines, Checkpoint 1. Options that customize the display of information. Copyright 2011 by CAST, Inc. All rights reserved. Used with permission.

To reinforce this knowledge, Module 2: Applying the UDL Framework to Lesson Development (*http://udlonline.cast.org*) is assigned as an independent practice activity. The module provides EDSP 422 students with the opportunity to examine their lesson plans within a UDL framework. This online tool critically examines potential barriers to student learning and recommends ways to eliminate these barriers with the assistance of digital media and other modifications. A culminating discussion question requires preservice teachers to synthesize their understanding of UDL and of how digital media can be used to increase content accessibility for a diverse student population.

Although the UDL lesson serves as the basis for how SSU supports preservice teachers in learning about and implementing UDL practices, the support extends beyond this specific lesson. Indeed, throughout the semester, EDSP 422 students are encouraged to share their experiences with and observations of UDL in the K–12 classroom. They typically report that they observe increased levels of student success and engagement in classrooms where teachers address diverse learning modalities and utilize authentic assessment measures that incorporate student choice. They discover that by using UDL in the classroom, teachers can offer their diverse learners options suited to their individual preferences and interests—options that continually engage their curiosity to learn.

A FORMER EDSP 422 STUDENT'S INTEGRATION OF UDL AND TECHNOLOGY IN THE SPECIAL EDUCATION CLASSROOM[1]

All teachers are challenged with questions of efficiency in their classrooms. How do I, as a teacher, impart the maximum amount of information to the maximum num-

---

[1] This section is written by Nick Wilson, a former EDSP 422 student.

ber of students in a limited time? How do I engineer instruction to meet the maximum number of individual needs? These questions grow more acute in classrooms that contain a significant percentage of students with learning disabilities. In some settings, there is a wide disparity in ability levels in the same classroom, which can further complicate matters.

The principles of UDL address the issues of creating accessibility for all. In the special education setting, students may have difficulties in comprehension through a particular sensory channel. Some students prefer to understand content through reading. For others, the visual channel is the most productive for taking in information. The resource specialist program setting in which I work magnifies these differences; however, they will occur in all classes to some extent. All individual students have optimal environmental and sensory conditions for information intake. Some students have analyzed their own learning preferences, but it is likely that most have not considered the issue in depth; they may only understand that they prefer one modality over another.

I have become an advocate at my school for the use of technology in the special education classrooms. It is not that I have a great infatuation with technology, but I see its use as something of a necessity, for the following reasons:

1. Computers can supply many of the Universal Access requirements of our students.
2. Their use can be adapted to the learning ability of each individual.
3. As a rule, there are great enthusiasm and aptitude for the use of computers in our population. Teachers should be leveraging, and students should be utilizing, their learning preferences.

Much of my teaching is enhanced by the use of visual aids projected through a liquid crystal display (LCD) projector connected to a computer, in response to my students' need for visual information. This vastly expands the curriculum base and increases students' attentiveness. I have found that the use of technology is enthusiastically embraced by the students. This is a generation that has grown up with the glowing screens of computer monitors, cell phones, and iPods. In effect, they have been conditioned every day to read and respond to material displayed on a lit monitor. The LCD monitor is used throughout the lesson to project workbook pages onto a whiteboard. Whiteboard markers are used to instruct the students on the lesson procedure. At the end of a particular lesson, a student volunteer fills out the page projected on the whiteboard, with input and assistance from the rest of the class.

Visuals, movie clips, audio clips, and current news stories can be integrated into the lesson to supplement understanding of a particular subject. At the end of each language class, the lights of the classroom are shut off, and a novel that has been previously scanned into the computer is projected onto the screen. The class members follow an oral reading by the teacher of the projected text in a way that they do not do when it is printed. A yardstick is used to point out the text being read. Toward the end of the chapter being read, the last few pages are handed out for the students to read independently. My language class is populated by students with the lowest reading ability in the school. As a generalization, this is a hard group to motivate to read anything; however, it is not an exaggeration to say that the students are all enthusiastically engaged in this type of reading. A few have become so enthusiastic that they have picked up the books from the library by themselves.

The lesson well illustrates my view of UDL in general. This is not something to be "plugged into" occasionally; rather, it is integrated into classroom procedures every day. A successful integration augments the lesson beyond addressing a few students' individual needs. These are some advantages of designing lessons that heavily incorporate visual information:

1. It is far more engaging to the majority of the class. Today's students see digital media as relevant media.
2. The dialogue can be easily expanded. For instance, a simple reading from a textbook on the history of art can be augmented with artwork from the web. My language students can now visually identify work by Diego Rivera, Alexander Calder, and some local graffiti heroes.
3. The amount of information in a well-prepared lesson can be many times greater. The pace of the class can also be faster, because of better and quicker understanding by the students.
4. Individual students' needs for alternative modalities are better met.

The last reason listed is, of course, the primary justification for UDL; however, the full implementation of UDL has much further-reaching consequences. As an example of an extension of the idea of creating a sensory-rich learning experience, I began a dialogue with some English teachers in which I requested that all assigned textbooks in the future have a readily available audio component available through all computers on campus. My students like to read a book while listening to it being read to them. The popularity of the practice among my students proves that it would be embraced by a greater population than only those diagnosed with specific learning disabilities.

THE INTERFACE BETWEEN UDL AND TECHNOLOGY: A CLASSROOM EXAMPLE

One example of how the principles of UDL are embedded in emerging educational technologies is the use of classroom-based amplification systems. Given that classrooms are highly dependent on hearing and speaking, the importance of being able to hear all forms of communication clearly cannot be underestimated (Edwards, 2005). When a classroom is equipped with a sound-field amplification system, the teacher's voice and the audio channels of various classroom technologies (TV, computer, DVD/MP3 players) are transmitted from small portable microphones to speakers located throughout the classroom that amplify voice or sound levels above the general room noise. When the teacher's voice and media sounds are amplified in this manner, all children (other than those with total or profound deafness) are provided with an equal opportunity to hear, regardless of seat location or the direction the teacher is facing (Millett, 2008). Although the concept of a sound-field system originated in the field of special education, researchers have identified more universal benefits of such systems:

- *Increased student attention:* Smaldino and Crandell (2000) reported benefits of classroom amplification for both student concentration and student attention span.
- *Increased student listening and auditory analysis:* Wilson, Marinac, Pitty, and Burrows (2011) found small but statistically significant improvements in student listening and auditory analysis in classrooms that were acoustically suited for the use of sound-field systems.
- *Improved student performance in general:* A longitudinal study by Gertel, McCarty, and Schoff (2004) found that students in amplified classrooms scored 10% better on a standardized achievement test than students in unamplified classrooms did.
- *Improved student performance for ELLs:* Researchers at the University of Florida (Crandell, 1996) tested the word perception of 20 native-Spanish-speaking students in classrooms with and without a sound-field system. Their findings revealed that these students understood up to 60% better in sound-field classrooms than in the nonamplified classrooms. Nelson, Kohnert, Sabur, and Shaw (2005) also report clear benefits of using amplification for ELLs.
- *Decreased teacher fatigue:* Massie and Dillon (2006) and Morrow and Connor (2011) report a significant reduction in teachers' overuse of their voices and general fatigue when sound-field systems were introduced in classroom settings.

The use of sound-field systems in classrooms addresses a diverse mix of students by enhancing and clarifying classroom audio. All students benefit from technologies that are flexible and integrated—and, in the end, such benefits accomplish the intent behind UDL. The following case study illustrates how this technology can become a powerful pedagogical support that not only reduces barriers to the learning process, but offers other educational benefits.

THE UDL–TECHNOLOGY INTERFACE: A CASE STUDY

Ashley H. is a third-grade teacher at H.V. Elementary School in Sonoma County, California. Since 2005, Ashley has had the opportunity to use a sound-field system in her classroom. Ashley's students mirror the overall school population: During the 2010–2011 school year, her 20 students included 3 students identified as deaf/hard of hearing (DHH); 3 with other learning differences (speech and language delays, reading disabilities, attentional difficulties); and several ELLs. Ashley was asked to consider the impact of the sound-field system on her classroom teaching.

How Did Ashley First Come to Use the Sound-Field System?

Ashley reported that her school adopted the sound-field system in phases. During the first phase, the sound-field system was installed in just a few classrooms as a pilot program to support students with mild hearing impairments. After 2 years, the school administrators noted that other students also benefited from the system, and they pursued additional funds to secure more sound-field systems across the school. As systems were installed in additional classrooms, students in the DHH program (other than those with total deafness) would routinely be placed in these equipped classrooms. Despite the fact that these placements may not have been based on sound pedagogical decisions, teachers noted that the placements did meet the students' assistive technology needs. Later, as the administrators continued to recognize the universal benefits of sound-field systems, the school launched a massive fund-raising effort that yielded enough capital to equip each classroom with its own sound-field system.

What Are the Benefits of a Sound-Field System for Students with Special Needs?

Ashley emphasized that her sound-field system does have clear benefits for students with disabilities. For students with mild hearing impairments, the system provides an increased opportunity to hear all teacher-directed instructions and lessons: Ashley noted, "I could be anywhere in the room, and they can hear me!" For students with more significant hearing impairments who use an FM system, the basic sound-field system may not sufficiently amplify Ashley's voice (this varies, depending upon the students' level of hearing loss), but she did note that the technology systems are very well integrated. In prior years, Ashley would have had to hear two microphones (one for the FM system and one for the sound-field system) in order to accommodate all her students' technology needs. Now the technology systems are integrated and flexible, so she can connect all technologies into the sound-field system in a seamless fashion.

What Are the Benefits to Other Students?

Ashley commented that students who are ELLs also benefit from the system. She reported that these students are able to hear her instructions and general English language usage more clearly, including proper articulation and intonation. She emphasized, however, that this is true for all students, in that they all now have the same opportunity to hear her communications. In other words, it offers everyone an opportunity to "sit in the front row." She has found that when she uses the system, she feels her students know that what she is saying is important. During the few recent times that she was not able to use her system (low batteries), she noted that her students seemed less engaged and interested. She commented on further benefits, including that her students really enjoy using the system themselves as they project their "teacher voices" across the classroom when they participate in a lesson or offer an answer to a question.

Are Any Other Benefits Noted?

In addition to the system's various benefits for the students, Ashley reported that her voice is less strained at the end of a typical day, now that she does not need to compete with the noise of the air conditioning, the hum of varied classroom equipment, and the general buzz within her classroom. Using a sound system helps minimize her need to project her "teacher voice" all day, which keeps her energy level up throughout the day. She emphasized that this was a wonderful unexpected benefit when she began to use her sound-field system.

What Would Ashley's Students Say about How This System Helps Them?

When prompted with a question concerning her students' feelings about the sound-field system, Ashley responded that most of her students are nontransitory and thus would likely not know the difference between a classroom with and one without such a system, given that they have been exposed to the technology since kindergarten. However, she did ask one student (Kami) who was a recent transfer from another school about her thoughts on the sound-field system in their classroom. Kami responded that although she had never seen this type of system before, she really did like how it worked. She also noted two specific benefits that had not previously occurred to Ashley. First, Kami noted that with the sound-field system she can distinguish between when her teacher is talking and when the other students are talking. For example, if the teacher says to "turn to page 32," then she knows that this is coming from the teacher and not the other students. Second, Kami noted that she is able to keep working on an assignment even when her teacher is talking. In her other classroom, she would have to look up and listen when the teacher was speaking, but now with the sound-field system she can keep working and not miss anything her teacher is saying.

How Did Ashley Sum Up Her Thoughts on Using a Sound-Field System?

Ashley concluded, "It's like this. . . . Students could sit in our classroom and use the natural light from the window to see what they are reading, but the students who sit near the window would obviously see better. Using a sound-field system is like turning the lights on: Everyone can 'see what they are reading' so much better."

MOVING FORWARD

We are in a unique period in American education—one that offers an unusual set of opportunities and challenges for preparing tomorrow's teachers to teach tomorrow's students. As we have seen, although current economic pressures are challenging, they also offer an opportunity for states and districts to critically examine their curricula and pedagogical practices. An increasingly diverse student population and a growing number of educational technologies are additional factors that must be considered as we explore how to provide a cost-effective, high-quality education for all students. UDL provides the conceptual framework for addressing the academic achievement needs of today's K–12 student population. The fact that this framework is now referenced in the federal HEOA with respect to teacher preparation programs is a testament to its widespread appeal.

The UDL Guidelines provide practical strategies for implementing UDL in instructional practice, including approaches for maximizing the inherent flexibility and cross-media richness of digital content and tools. Capitalizing on technology use to increase achievement opportunities for all students corresponds to the rapid permeation of technology into consumer culture: In both cases, we are seeing a rapid increase in Web 2.0 collaborations; online learning; multimedia creation and access via smartphones and other mobile devices; the proliferation of digital text; and the decline of print as the predominant medium. Each of these changes carries with it enormous and transformative potential, along with certain risks. Perhaps the biggest challenge for those in the position of training future educators is the development of programs that are both valid and effective, while maintaining a high degree of openness to the continuing cultural shifts that will undoubtedly occur.

Future teachers working in 21st-century classrooms face an increasingly diverse student body, ongoing curriculum reforms, and rapid educational technology advances. Teacher preparation programs that successfully integrate UDL experiences in meaningful and relevant ways offer their candidates a framework for how to consider and address these factors as they strive to meet the educational needs of all their students.

REFERENCES

California Department of Education (CDE). (2011). *Student and school data reports.* Sacramento, CA: Author. Retrieved February 24, 2012, from *http://www.cde.ca.gov/ds/sd/sd.*

CAST. (2011). *Universal Design for Learning Guidelines version 2.0.* Wakefield, MA: Author. Retrieved from *http://www.udlcenter.org/aboutudl/udlguidelines.*

Commission on Teacher Credentialing. (2009). *California standards for the teaching profession.* Sacramento, CA: Author. Retrieved February 24, 2012, from *http://www.ctc.ca.gov/educator-prep/standards/CSTP-2009.pdf.*

Coyne, P., Pisha, B., Dalton, B., Zeph, L. A., & Cook Smith, N. (2010, August). Literacy by design: A Universal Design for Learning approach for students with significant intellectual disabilities. *Remedial and Special Education.* Retrieved September 30, 2010, from *http://rse.sagepub.com/content/early/2010/08/30/0741932510381651.*

Crandell, C. (1996). Effects of sound field FM amplification on the speech perception of ESL children. *Education Audiology Monographs, 4,* 1–5.

Edwards, D. (2005). A formative evaluation of sound field amplification system across several grade levels in four schools. *Journal of Educational Audiology, 12,* 59–66.

Gertel, S. J., McCarty, P. J., & Schoff, L. (2004). High performance schools equals high performing students. *Educational Facility Planner, 39,* 20–24.

Higher Education Opportunity Act (HEOA). (2008, August 14). Public Law 110-315. Retrieved from *http://www2.ed.gov/policy/highered/leg/hea08/index.html.*

Massie, R., & Dillon, H. (2006). The impact of sound-field amplification in mainstream cross-cultural classrooms: Part 2. Teacher and child opinions. Retrieved January 23, 2011, from *http://www.accessmylibrary.com/article-1G1-144351368/impact-sound-field-amplification. html.*

Means, B., Toyama, Y., Murphy, R., Bakia, M., & Jones, K. (2009). *Evaluation of evidence-based practices in online learning: A meta-analysis and review of online learning studies.* Washington, DC: U.S. Department of Education.

Millett, P. (2008). Sound field amplification research summary. Retrieved January 23, 2011, from *http://gofrontrow.com/files/documents/research/sound-field-amplification-research-summary. pdf.*

Morrow, S. L., & Connor, N. P. (2011). Voice amplification as a means of reducing vocal load for elementary music teachers. *Journal of Voice, 25*(4), 441–446.

Nelson, P., Kohnert, K., Sabur, S., & Shaw, D. (2005). Classroom noise and children learning a second language: Double jeopardy. *Language, Speech, and Hearing Services in Schools, 36*(3), 219–229.

Picciano, A. G., & Seaman, J. (2009, January). K–12 online learning: A 2008 follow-up of the survey of U.S. school district administrators. The Sloan Consortium. Retrieved March 6, 2009, from *http://www.sloanconsortium.org/publications/survey/pdf/k-12_online_learning_ 2008.pdf.*

Rose, D., & Meyer, A. (2002). *Teaching every student in the digital age: Universal Design for Learning.* Alexandria, VA: Association for Supervision and Curriculum Development.

Smaldino, J., & Crandell, C. (2000). Classroom amplification technology: Theory and practice. *Language, Speech, and Hearing Services in Schools, 3,* 371–375.

Wilson, W. J., Marinac, J., Pitty, K., & Burrows, C. (2011). The use of sound-field amplification devices in different types of classrooms. *Language Speech, and Hearing Services in Schools, 42,* 395–407.

Index